MW00981823

Have More Fun!

Have More Fun!

Bob Wood

Condor Books
Novato, California

Have More Fun!

Condor Books
Publishers Services
P.O. Box 2510
Novato, CA 94948
FAX (415) 883-4280

Printed in the United States of America

Cover and book design by Paula Morrison and Catherine Campaigne

ISBN: 0-913238-05-8

 For my wife Deanne, a constant source of delight and my accomplice in fun.

For researcher John Boeschen who mined the scant literature of fun for me.

For book designers Paula Morrison and Catherine Campaigne who creatively added visual fun to the package.

And for all the many friends and acquaintances and strangers who encouraged me to help them get more fun out of life.

Table of Contents

What's IN This Book?

Are you having enough fun? Or do you suffer from Fun Deficiency, Fun Deprivation, Fun Starvation, Fun Anemia? You do if you go more than a few hours without fun. Three times an hour is more like it! It's never too late to let fun into your life. It's eagerly waiting just around the corner, barely out of sight, within the reach of all of us. All you have to do is choose to let fun in.

Have More Fun! will bring it rushing back in a hurry. Within hours you'll have more fun than you've probably had in weeks—maybe years! Fun comes back fast if you give it half a chance, because it's your birthright, the bottom line of life. Your highest aspiration is the hope—beyond success—of enjoying unlimited fun! Deep down—like little kids—we just want to have fun.

Have More Fun! is built on the premise that FUN, like love—and great sex—lives in your head.

Real fun—the long-lasting, richly rewarding, always ready, safe, and dependable, deeply satisfying kind that's guaranteed to lift your life—is an attitude, a viewpoint, a state of mind, a way of looking at life. Real fun comes from an appreciation of the moment, spontaneous playfulness, a humorous orientation, a frolicsome outlook, an antic mood, an inclination toward amusement, the ability to laugh at the world—and yourself.

So, finding fun simply means changing your feelings, attitudes and beliefs. That's the theme of this book.

In *Have More Fun!* you learn to change feelings three ways:

1. By unblocking the principal barriers to fun—pessimism, worry, doubt, anxiety, frustration, pressure, stress, guilt, fear, undeservability, and the various fun-killing strictures of society.

2. By employing instant fun-generating, crackup physical techniques that both re-discover fun and help you express it.

3. By learning to develop the self-esteem, optimism, self trust, desire, expectation, and self-worth that dependably lead to real fun.

Along the way you'll discover the many exciting benefits that having more fun can confer—relaxation, better sleep, weight loss, popularity, better health, contentment—and success of every kind. Experts present supporting medical, psychological, metaphysical and scientific evidence of fun's virtues. Fun is both the end and the means of success.

A short history documents the demise of "Original Fun" and the resultant poisoning of western civilization. "Fun on the Job" shows how to turn work into play. Adding fun to sex puts the play back in foreplay. Plus dynamite advanced techniques for deliberately creating more fun and success for the rest of your life.

So come on! Lighten up! And let the fun begin!

"The one serious conviction a
man should hold is that nothing ...
be taken too seriously."
Samuel Butler

Preface

Who is this Guy, Wood?

Maybe I'm peculiar but when I'm reading a book, I want to know a lot about the author. I turn again and again to those pitiful few lines written by some publicist who has probably never met her—trying to assess her credentials, wondering what she's really like. I want to know how successful she's been as a person. Can I trust her? Does she practice what she preaches? What are her qualifications?

So I'm going to tell you quite a lot about myself, so you can judge my credentials for writing a book about fun,

What kind of guy am I? I'll start with what I'm not. I'm not an academic, physician, therapist, or psychologist. I'm not a mystic, astrologer, clairvoyant, or psychic. I try not to get too serious about anything—including growth and fun. I used to see myself as some kind of intellectual—until I realized that it wasn't much fun.

I'm an ordinary guy who watches Monday night football, drinks a little beer, and plays basketball and tennis ... for the fun of it. I'm an introvert who's been a forest ranger and a river guide. I love to travel and walk in the wilds. I also like to sing, dance, laugh, eat, play with animals and kids, paint, swim, be with my friends, travel, daydream and meet stimulating people. But most of all I love to have fun.

Fun has done a lot for me. I have a wonderful life and I'm moderately successful in a variety of areas. I seem to have more fun than most people, and that's a big part, I'm convinced, of my success. At this writing I'm 64, a trim five-foot-ten and 145 pounds. Being a self-employed writer and financially independent, I can do what I want.

I used to be a feisty, combative, serious basketball and tennis player (with the sprains and broken bones to prove it), until I finally realized—after only forty years!—that fierce competition wasn't much fun. Nowadays I'm content to put on imaginary exhibitions with Michael Jordan, and two minutes after playing tennis I've forgotten who won.

Success as an investor in rundown real estate allowed me to "retire" at age 34 from a wonderful job as *Life Magazine* Correspondent in San Francisco. Ten years later, I retired again, this time from active management of my investments. By then, I had a wife and daughter, a lovely home, a cabin in the mountains, money in the bank and the leisure to travel and write books—everything I'd always wanted. So how come I wasn't really happy? Where was the freedom and fun I'd worked hard for? Maybe authorship would bring it.

But after writing several successful outdoor books, with no discernible increase in happiness, I started more actively searching for fun. When friends exposed me to Primal Therapy, I was ripe for something new. My journal of that profound experience became a book entitled *Good-bye, Loneliness!* (Dell, 1974). In it I tried to explain the transformation, part physical, part emotional, part mental, that brought me a peace and contentment I'd never known.

I quickly regained my lost ability to feel and to express my feelings, spontaneously and naturally, the way a child does.

Miraculously, my body became looser, my voice became deeper, and my normal body temperature dropped. I laughed and cried easily, my mind became clearer. I was alert, relaxed, and beginning to have fun.

But that was twenty years ago. Let's go back to the beginning. I was born in 1930 in Berkeley, California, the son of a hard-driving civil engineer father and a loving artist mother. I was highly allergic, but my mother lavished a lot of love on her sick baby, so I started life secure and content. As a little boy, I loved to sit in the garden by the fishpond, watching the goldfish and the butterflies, but gradually the demands of school, parents and church stole my fun. I grew up sickly, allergic, small for my age, timid, introverted, and shy.

Every week I went to Sunday school where I was taught humility and obedience, to think of others before myself. At the time those selfless beliefs seemed reasonable, even noble. I couldn't see that I was giving up a vital part of myself, handing over my power, denying self love. I never dreamed that I was headed for shame and guilt, instead of the fun I'd experienced as a child.

In high school I enjoyed minor success in sports and music, and began to study singing. My mother pressed me to take classes from her minister and become a member of her church. But the minister and my classmates seemed embarrassed by my innocent questions, and it was politely suggested that I "wasn't quite ready" to join.

Like my father before me, I went to the University of California, where my love of the outdoors led me to major in Forestry. I joined a fraternity but soon led a pledge class revolt and resigned in protest over dishonest, cruel, and immoral policies. My happiest hours were spent singing with the Glee Club, where my voice training got me solos in musicals and shows. I graduated in 1952 with the lowest grade point average in the history of the College of Forestry, and set off on a tramp steamer to see Europe, financed by money I had made the summer before working in a construction camp kitchen in the arctic.

On the boat, I met two boys my age on their way to Fulbright and Rhodes Scholarships at Cambridge and Oxford. We became friends and decided to travel together. All summer long as we traipsed through Europe, they talked of nothing but their passion for writing. By the time I returned to Berkeley in the fall, I too had decided to become a writer.

Three months earlier I had boasted about getting through college without taking a course in English. Now I naively asked the University's placement center for a job as a writer. A month later, I got a call. A San Francisco publisher was looking for a young editor. One by one it had rejected the School of Journalism's entire crop of eager graduates. The publisher, it turned out, hated journalism schools, so I got the job. At 22, I was the youngest, cockiest, most ignorant editor in the city.

Within months in my spare time, I started writing my first book, a narrative account of my backpacking/trout fishing trips into the High Sierra wilderness. It was never published. A year later, I decided I was wasting my talent as a mere editor. I would become another Hemingway. So I quit my job and went to Mexico to write sensitive short stories.

None of these were published, so when I ran out of money, I came back to Berkeley to live in a garret, still grimly writing bad fiction. I got by on a series of part-time jobs as a book reviewer, editor of a fishing and hunting weekly, free lance travel writer … anything. Throughout my twenties I was hypersensitive, love-starved, and unhappy. Fun was never farther away.

Just before I turned thirty, my luck suddenly changed. In the space of a year I got a full time job editing the University's alumni magazine, married Freda, a fellow editor, wrote a few articles for the San Francisco office of *Time, Life,* and *Sports*

Illustrated and bought my first investment property. But in less than a year I was fired by my jealous boss at the alumni journal for publishing stories in national magazines. To my surprise and delight, my new friends at Time, Inc. supplied me with a full time job as a reporter.

Two years later, Random House gave me a contract to expand a *Life* story I had written about an old prospector into a book. I wrote the book but when I refused to make alterations that I felt weren't honest, it was rejected.

Three years later—by now I was the San Francisco *Life* correspondent—my boss in Los Angeles asked me to write a story that I felt defamed innocent people. When I refused, he took me off the story and wrote it himself. Against his orders, I wrote my own version and teletyped it to the magazine's editors in New York. They published my story instead of his. When he vowed revenge, it was time to take stock.

My real estate investments were beginning to make money and a book publisher had offered me a lucrative contract to write a series of books, each a company history. So I quit Time, Inc. and started writing about a giant seed producer. But it soon became clear that I was supposed to bend the facts to glorify the company, so once again I quit.

All through my youth I had been sickly and allergic. It wasn't until college that I outgrew my asthma and food allergies. But hay fever persisted, requiring allergy shots every three weeks. Soon after I left Time, Inc., a friend pointed me to a chiropractic internist who had helped a lot of people. Within a month, Dr. William A. Nelson, D.C. had dispatched many of my worst symptoms. Two months later, holding my breath, I skipped my allergy shot for the first time in ten years. The sky didn't fall and I never went back for another.

During that time, I was far too busy painting apartments, cleaning toilets and mowing lawns to think of writing. There was a mountain of work and no money to hire help. Then I met a realtor who helped me trade my little apartment houses into bigger ones. By the time I was forty, I was out of the woods financially and ready to try another book.

Five years before, I had bought a falling-down mountain cabin, accessible only by boat or trail, on the edge of Desolation Wilderness, high in the California Sierra. Using it as a base, I set about systematically exploring the 200-square mile wilderness, producing a detailed guidebook that was published in 1970. I was finally an author, but somehow it wasn't the thrill I had expected.

But backpacking was starting to boom so I spent two years writing a comprehensive "How to." *Pleasure Packing* was instantly an underground bestseller, and that winter I took my family to New Zealand and Australia on the profits. A phrase from the introduction to that book now seems prophetic: "... our ultimate goal is simply to have fun." My next book was *Mountain Cabin,* a Thoreauian love letter to my Walden in the Sierra. But the satisfaction didn't last and soon I was searching for greener fields.

That's when I discovered primal therapy—and a need for more fun in my life. Many of the fun-releasing techniques in chapters five through eight had their origins in primal and feeling therapy. Making use of my new ability to express feelings, I took up oil painting, instructed by my artist mother. In the space of two years I had three one-man shows, and sold more than half my work. Then my publisher asked me to write another book (*The 2 oz. Backpacker*), so I put away my paints, but I designed the cover and produced a dozen drawings to illustrate the text. By now I was beginning to have a little fun.

When Freda and I amicably divorced, I found myself alone in a home I had built in the desert for our retirement. It sat on an island in the wild West Walker River in a beautiful but remote mile-high valley on the California-Nevada border. The culture shock was numbing and I was terribly lonely—until friends talked me into a raft trip 225 miles down the Colorado River. I came back hooked on whitewater rafting, determined to become a river guide. I got my first job guiding at the age of 52 and wrote a book called *Whitewater Boatman, The Making of a River Guide.*

On one of those trips I met a recently divorced young school teacher from the Nevada desert, with a 3-year old daughter named Angela. Deanne had never lived in the city—and wasn't about to start. We promptly fell in love. She saw no obstacle in the twenty year difference in our ages, so we were married in a Mexican restaurant at a dusty crossroads in the desert. Now I had a willing travel and hiking companion. We bought a bungalow in a tiny village in Hawaii, where we lived the winter half of the year. Life was definitely getting better.

But every autumn in the desert my pollen allergies made life unbearable. When the rabbit brush and sage were in bloom, I was forced into exile. Then I heard about homeopathy and Hahnemann Clinic in Berkeley. A doctor there named Bill Gray told me he could cure my allergies—and everything else that my body perceived as an affliction. It would take three years but homeopathic remedies were safe and holistic. I was ready.

Bill Gray turned out to be America's foremost homeopath, and he happened to own several of my books. He offered to open all the doors if I wanted to write one on homeopathy. Before a year had passed, Deanne was treating minor ailments homeopathically for our family and friends, and I was writing an introductory book for the general public. *Homeopathy, Medicine That Works!* was published in 1990.

Just as Bill forecast, three years after taking a single homeopathic remedy, my allergy was gone. I didn't have to hide out from the pollen any longer. Even better, my lifelong irritability declined. The relief was enormous. Suddenly, life was a lot more fun!

Hiking in Hawaii I found a book in a wrecked car that sharply changed our eating habits. It was *Fit For Life* by Harvey and Marilyn Diamond. To pass along our discoveries, I included a chapter on its benefits in my 1991 book, *Dayhiker, Walking for Fitness, Fun & Adventure.* There's also a chapter entitled, "Homeopathy Revolutionizes First Aid in the Wilds."

Eight years ago came by far the biggest breakthrough in my search for fun, turning my groping quest into a conscious and deliberate pursuit. Philosophical exploring finally led me to beliefs that accessed the fun and joy I'd been seeking. Applying the power of deliberate thought to summon fun and success has turned my life around. Nowadays, an hour rarely passes without the magnificent leavening of fun.

So there you have it, a glimpse of my life—so you can judge my credentials for writing this book about fun. I hope it helps you get more fun out of life.

> *In* One Flew Over the Cuckoo's Nest, *a Ken Kesey character says, "You have to laugh at the things that hurt to keep the world from running you plumb crazy."*

Introduction

Why Fun?

Individually, we yearn for fun, but collectively, we deny and disparage it. Everybody talks about it, but nobody quite knows how to find it—and keep it. We're secretly ashamed that we've settled for a life without much fun. We don't want to be reminded of how much fun we're missing—because it hurts. Sadly, we're conspirators in the denial of fun, turning our backs on what ought to be our highest aspiration—the hope (beyond success) of enjoying unlimited fun.

We say, "Fun's just for kids," while secretly we covet it. Society condescendingly looks down on fun as frivolous, shallow, selfish, and unworthy. When we're lucky enough to possess it even momentarily, we get vaguely uneasy—even feel a little guilty. Too much fun, we recall, is somehow bad—although we can't remember exactly why. So we helplessly participate in a conspiracy of denial, and fragile fun disappears from our serious busy lives.

The notion of taking fun seriously evokes all kinds of violent reactions, from angry denial to ardent desire. The subject turns out to be as sensitive as sex. More than a few workaholic literary agents and publishers responded to my queries by flatly declaring, "We don't see a market for a book about fun!"

Institutionally, fun is frowned on, because it represents real freedom and independence—which threaten authority of every kind (parents, teachers, employers, the church and state). "They" don't want you to have too much fun. They won't say why. It's just not permitted! Fun hasn't been respectable in our culture since the Protestant work ethic put out the lights five centuries ago.

America in the nineties is clearly starved for fun. The evidence is overwhelming. We're the freest of nations—yet one of the most repressed. But that's beginning to change. The Dark Ages are lifting and fun is making a timid comeback. Hard-hearted business has discovered that fun pays. The pleasure industry is booming, and employee fun has become high priority for enlightened business management.

A recent PBS special showed captains of industry cavorting at a seminar to learn the benefits of fun in the workplace—because workers allowed a little fun on the job turn out to be significantly more creative, productive, and loyal to the company. Fun is the latest management tool.

Making people happy is a billion dollar industry, and not just in America. Disneylands and fun theme parks are springing up all over the world. The Paris Disneyland, when complete, will be a fifth the size of that fun-famous city. Mickey Mouse is a universal symbol of fun. The fun revolution has circled the globe.

Over 85 percent of the movies shown in Europe are American, because Hollywood knows how to bring alive the wealth, celebrity, happiness, and hope that add up to fun for millions of fun-starved people worldwide. And it's the same in other countries. America's fun-oriented lifestyle has aroused the world's yearning for freedom and opportunity—and the fervent hope of somehow finding fun. The word is out: you can fight back with fun.

Television and teenagers ("It's *so* fun, man!"), those harbingers of fad and fashion, have recently discovered fun and made it their own. On the tube, the billboards, on radio, and in print, beautiful people are assuring us, "It's okay to have fun." Fun is now the buzzword for selling nearly everything. ("Take a break for pure mindless fun," says Pepsi). Clearly, fun is inching out of the closet.

Of course, a lot of this new fun is phony—empty, short-lived, shallow, and unhealthy. But don't worry about that. We'll show you the real thing, the right stuff, the deeply satisfying, always ready, long lasting, richly rewarding kind of fun that's guaranteed to lift your life. If you're ready for fun, it's waiting just around the corner, barely out of sight, within the reach of all of us—no matter how wretched and depressed we may feel.

Have More Fun! isn't for everybody. But if you're ready to allow more fun into your life, this book will bring back the magic, helping you reclaim fun's joyful allure, leading you home to its warmth and good feelings. Hilarious, crackup physical techniques will give you a taste of fun in a matter of minutes. Within hours you'll have more fun than you've probably had in weeks—maybe years! Fun comes back fast when you give it half a chance—because it belongs.

Along the way you'll learn to fight fear with fun, turn pessimism into optimism, break fun-killing habits, ditch depressing worry, and reduce your dependency on the opinion of others. And you'll learn to breach the barriers that block fun from your life. All you need is the desire for more fun in your life, and the belief that you're entitled to unlimited fun, as long as it doesn't hurt anyone else. And our kind doesn't.

The catchy Bobby Ferrin tune that rhythmically repeats, "Don' worry, be happy!" delivers the right message but doesn't show you how. We will.

Employing an eclectic collection of proven techniques, we

take you by the hand and lead you down the path, showing you how to change your feelings and reclaim lost fun.

Whether your goal is serious therapy or carefree frivolity— success, relaxation or merely more amusement—the surefire strategies that follow will bring you back to fun again.

So kick back, lighten up, and let the fun begin!

Bob Wood

Tahoe Paradise, CA
June, 1995

1

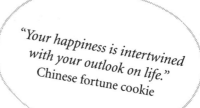

> "Your happiness is intertwined with your outlook on life."
> Chinese fortune cookie

What Fun Can Do

"**A**re we having fun yet?" roars the party animal, guffawing. Probably not. Like most people, he's missing out on real fun. But the sad familiar question reveals prevailing attitudes, hinting at our yearning—and our embarrassment—about wanting more fun in our lives. Nevertheless, we doggedly pursue it because we know that it's somehow essential to our happiness. Deep down, instinctively, we *know* we need fun.

Modern science confirms it. Recent studies show fun is the secret ingredient in conjuring success of every kind, the medicine that cures all manner of afflictions. It can lift you to new happiness and freedom. Fun is the key that gets you out of jail. Time flies when you're having fun. You look and feel better, relate better, work better. People like people who know how to have fun because they're totally alive and fun to be with.

Real fun is the ultimate high because having fun *is* fun! There's no pleasanter therapy, no sweeter medicine. Having fun feels wonderful! Fun releases the brake that's been holding you back. It's stimulating and exciting, and best of all it's free. Real fun doesn't cost a penny. The Good Life is measured by how much fun you're having, not how many toys you possess.

Fun is a catalyst. It turns lead into gold, it turns work into play, and makes everything easier and more enjoyable. Add more fun to your life and you change love, work, relationships—everything! Things go better with fun—*especially* work. Like rose-colored glasses, fun transforms everything you see. And it's mercifully independent of who you are, what you're doing, who you're with, or where you are.

Fun is a lifespring, a safety net, a survival system, the partner of hope. This magnificent tool can unlock any door, heal any disease, even rescue you from death, because fun is essential to life. It's the birthright of every one of us, the bottom line of life. Where there's life there's hope—the hope of having fun again!

"Life is not life without delight," says the poet. Every other goal is just a means to that end. No wonder wise men through the ages have cultivated fun, cherishing it as a noble end in itself. They insist that we were born to have fun. Some say it's our reason for living!

What Fun Can Do

Fun can raise self-esteem, stimulate creativity, end loneliness, win promotions, attract new friends, promote clarity, build your sense of humor, cure addictions of all kinds, dissolve anger, improve health, deflect hostility, ward off illness, lengthen life, reduce stress, ease tension and anxiety, fight depression, repair sagging relationships, boost optimism and self esteem, improve sleep, raise job satisfaction, build personal appeal, stimulate creativity, promote relaxation—even enhance sex.

Everything goes better if you make it into fun. Nowhere is fun more valuable than in the workplace, where it can actually turn work into play. That's why big business is getting serious about fun, spending big bucks to make work more appealing because workers who have fun are more productive, loyal, and creative. And there isn't any downside. You simply can't have too much fun, not if it's the genuine article.

Real vs. Phony Fun

But there's a world of difference between real fun and the phony, beer ad facsimile we see every hour on television. Phony fun—shrill hilarity, frantic action, quick romance and easy sex—is empty, shallow, and short-lived. Real fun is rich, deeply satisfying, and relaxing.

What is real fun? It's an attitude, a way of seeing, a happy outlook on life. It's a playful inclination, a talent for amusement, appreciation of the moment, looking on the bright side, seeing the humor, finding merriment and mirth. It's smiling when you're down, laughing at yourself. It's clowning, joking, talking nonsense, playfulness, foolishness, being tickled, singing, humming, dancing, smiling, laughing, rhyming, punning, unbridled optimism. Real fun is almost anything you do—if you do it happily, joyfully, spontaneously, with pleasure.

Since fun lives in your head, it's always ready and waiting, dependable and safe. No one can steal it. You can turn it on at will by simply changing your feelings. And fun can be learned. You don't need a shrink to tap into its magic. Most of the time you don't even need to change what you're doing. Just change your feelings so you have fun doing it. That's the theme of this book.

Fun is a viewpoint, a way of looking at the world. (And, as a wise man once said, "Point of view is *every*thing.") Fun is the expression of love and affection. It's independent of time and place, it doesn't matter where you are or what you're doing. It doesn't require leisure, friends, or tripping off to some romantic hideaway. You don't have to laugh or even smile, although it helps.

Nowadays "fun" has many negative connotations. To distinguish real fun from the phony variety, let's consider what it's not. Real fun isn't poking fun, crude jokes, sarcasm with a smile, needling, irony, or practical jokes. It isn't ridicule, cruelty, playing tricks, malicious teasing, excessive tickling, or deliberate embarrassment. It's not playing the fool, taking pratfalls, or making fun of others.

That's the good news. Unfortunately, fun has many enemies, especially in high places. There are five distinct barriers that block the path to unlimited fun.

Fun's Five Enemies

First come its enemies within and without.

1. The Enemy Within, like fun, lives inside our heads. The worry, doubt, anxiety, frustration and pressure that muddle our brains also block fun from our serious lives. Our lifetime supply of hangups, neuroses, and negative beliefs keep fun low priority.

2. The Enemy Without is society itself. Parents, schools, the church, and state—institutions of every kind—are threatened by fun because it offers an independence that undermines obedience to authority. Society tells us fun is foolish and frivolous, immature, irresponsible, and fit only for children.

3. Little wonder that we're afraid of being caught seeking fun. We're self-conscious, embarrassed and uneasy with fun. Too much of it dependably triggers shame, guilt, and anxiety.

4. Not surprisingly, we've forgotten what fun looks like and how to find it. We're rusty, awkward, out of practice. We don't know how to find fun anymore.

5. Fun is fragile, elusive. Doubt and worry send frail fun scampering from sight, like a timid rabbit diving down its hole—leaving a sad sterile seriousness behind. The slightest hint of trouble and fragile fun is gone.

With this minefield to cross, no wonder real fun is so scarce. No wonder most of us suffer from fun deficiency, fun deprivation, and fun anemia. Fortunately there are models of pure fun to serve as teachers: children.

Kids Know All About Fun

Wise men insist that we were born to have fun. They say it's our primary purpose in life. All of us were born knowing how to have fun. Infants all possess it. Babies come into the world with the talent. Sadly, as we grow up, we somehow lose the knack, but for the young it's as easy as breathing. Effortlessly and instinctively, babies coo and gurgle with delight. In a month they can smile, in six months they're laughing. As long as they're comfortable, life is unalloyed fun.

Little children, too, are models of fun, geniuses at play, experts at amusing themselves. Innocently uninhibited, they reach for what they want, always seeking fun. They haven't learned to worry or care what others think. All they want is fun, so they're experts at finding it, anywhere and everywhere. They don't need toys or adult supervision. Fun lives in their hearts; it's their constant companion.

Why do babies and kids have so much fun? Because they don't analyze or doubt or wonder what people think. They aren't beset with worries. They don't take their values from society. They just think of themselves and follow their urges and unashamedly pursue fun full-time. That's why they make such wonderful role models. By observing kids at play and copying what they do we can rediscover fun for ourselves.

Sadly, our youthful love affair with fun doesn't last. We grow up and learn to worry. Fun begins to fade when parents begin to scold and make demands. Then the schools take over, teaching us shame, obedience, doubt, and dignity. Next the church steps in, requiring duty and devotion. Finally we're assaulted by the prejudice and mores of society itself. The fear, obedience, and control in our culture kills off the last of our fun. Individually, we still seek it, but collectively—as society—we join the conspiracy to ridicule, thwart, subvert, and destroy it. Our institutions don't want us too happy or too free. Authority is threatened by fun.

The dictionary definition of "selfish" reveals the sad attitudes prevailing in our culture. "Selfish," we're told means "... excessively self concerned, without regard for others." We tremble at the thought of being seen as selfish, because the sin of selfishness is swiftly punished by embarrassment, guilt and shame. It's taken to mean cruel, hurtful, mean and unkind. But most of us desperately need to be *more* selfish—in the sense of the word that concerns our "own well-being, pleasure and welfare."

It's hard to hang onto fun while growing up. Wistfully, we turn our backs, telling ourselves that fun is just for kids. We accept the grim prescription that "growing up" means saying goodbye to fun and play. We accept the cold comfort of duty, devotion, and responsibility. Society helps by inflicting guilt, shame, and embarrassment on those who dare to play in a serious world. Fun, we are told, is chaos. We must submit to order. So we give up our fun, often never knowing the tragedy of our loss.

But deep inside we still crave fun. It's a universal longing, a fundamental yearning, our ultimate ambition. We want it back because deep in our bones we know it's the best thing we ever had. The fun in our lives makes up our best memories. For some of us, it's the only good thing that ever happened. We're haunted by fun, starved for it. Though we try to conceal it, especially from ourselves, we live in the secret hope of some-day having fun.

Once it's gone, we spend the rest of our lives striving vain-ly to recapture it—directly or (more often) indirectly, some-times consciously but usually unconsciously. We sleepwalk through life, forever chasing rainbows, hunting for fun with-out much success. We stubbornly pursue it because somehow we know we need it to survive.

Fortunately, fun never dies. It just goes dormant, waiting to be revived. We never really lose it because it's part of the mys-terious force that keeps us alive. Like hope, it survives as long as we do. So it's never too late to resurrect fun. It's buried some-where deep within the most hopeless of us, patiently waiting, like the genie in the bottle, to be released. The memory of fun is embedded in our genes. Our bodies remember, and they're ready to welcome it back, if we'll let them.

We're Desperate for Fun

Despite the glitzy ads that try to depict it, fun has never been so scarce. The best barometer of our lack is the alarming rise of depression in America. Studies show that severe depression is ten times more prevalent now than it was fifty years ago. It afflicts twice as many women as men, and it man-ifests a full decade earlier in life than it did only twenty years ago.

"Depression is the common cold of mental illness," says psy-chologist Martin E. P. Seligman. Fully a quarter of Americans suffer from "normal" depression, and severe manic-depressive states are also on the rise. Millions of women poison their bod-ies continuously with anti-depressant drugs. And more than a million have risked surgical breast implants in the vain hope that a more voluptuous body will somehow bring more fun.

Other statistics paint a fun-starved picture of America in the nineties.

We spend more than seven hours a day passively watching television, but commuting fathers can only find seven minutes a day to spend with their children. The divorce rate has more than doubled in the last half century. Drug arrests are up 350 percent since 1980. In the last ten years, child abuse has risen 325 percent. Children are dropping out of school and running away from home, turning to drugs and sex earlier and in greater numbers. Teenage rape, murder, pregnancy, and suicide are all on the rise, telling us kids aren't having much fun, either.

The grim 19th century indictment, "Most men lead lives of quiet desperation," has never been so true. One study shows that Americans live in a state of low grade anxiety a shocking 90 percent of the time. The incidence of rape rose 59 percent in 1991 alone. Insomnia and heartburn are steeply rising, as shown by the sales figures of the largely ineffective medicines being prescribed to combat them. Violent crime, both in the streets and in our homes, is steadily climbing.

There's been a steady rise in the suicide rate, the homicide rate, homelessness, school dropouts, child abuse, random violence and addictions of all kinds. Education and skill levels are steadily dropping. Patchwork solutions blindly address the symptoms while ignoring the causes. More cops, bigger prisons, tougher laws and stricter teachers aren't helping. Our culture is in steep decline, along with our environment.

America's health is rapidly deteriorating. Genuine cure of illness is increasingly rare, and most over the counter drugs bring only mild temporary relief. We spend a shockingly high 12 percent of our GNP on medicines, but wonder drugs are growing less effective and more dangerous every year, putting more and more people in the hospital—or the morgue. AIDS, cancer, heart disease, hypertension, allergies, and chronic maladies of all kinds are on the increase.

We've sacrificed fun to a Promethean preoccupation with speed, efficiency, and productivity. Our hurry-up culture is increasingly ruled by an impatient, computer-compulsive time ethic in which our environment is increasingly contrived and artificial. As society grows more manipulative and controlled, the individual is increasingly isolated and dehumanized. There's never enough time, no way to relax. As we race down the fast track at an ever more frantic pace, we're stressed by a sea of speeded-up technology devoid of all feeling.

In short, we're not having much fun. Finding fun again can take us through the looking glass to escape the stress of accelerated time.

Our desperate yearning for fun has spawned a multi-million dollar pleasure and relaxation industry offering garish, manic, artificial experience. But the pleasure has proved to be empty and short-lived, and true relaxation still manages to elude us. No matter what we do or where we go, we can't seem to really relax.

The Secret of Real Relaxation

Relaxation is a major quest of the nineties. In search of it we drink, take drugs, travel, take up fads, spend money, turn to sex, go into therapy, fight for leisure, take courses, overeat, read how-to books, watch comedians and funny movies, buy leisure toys, undergo cosmetic surgery, globetrot, meditate, take vitamins, diet, join gyms and more—all in a vain attempt to escape pressure, restlessness, tension, boredom, and stress.

Most of these relaxation strategies don't work well, or for very long because they fail to recognize that relaxation, like fun, is a state of mind. It has nothing to do with where you are, who you're with, or what you're doing. Experts agree that real relaxation comes from real change. But what do you change—and how?

Why not try a change in attitude and outlook? Why not try fun! Unlike other strategies, it requires no money, time, or space. Just switch from seriousness to the pursuit of real fun. Real relaxation is waiting—in your head. It's nothing more than an attitude, and *anyone* can learn it. And fun is the best teacher. Having fun is the secret of real relaxation.

The Fun Diet

Sixty million Americans admit they're overweight. Forty million have tried dieting, further (ironic) evidence of fun starvation. Many unhappy people overeat, then feel guilty about the resulting fat. They equate feeling full and stimulating their taste buds with the missing pleasure they crave. Fun can break the cycle, offering an alternative to overeating.

Here's our recipe. If you're feeling dissatisfied and find yourself heading for the refrigerator or the candy counter, take a fun break instead and watch the pounds melt away. To prepare yourself for an attack of the munchies, just draw up a short list of diversions that dependably produce fun and pick the activity that best fits your present circumstance. Then, instead of eating, generate two minutes of distracting, entertaining, uplifting, no-calorie fun. The need for food will vanish, and your happiness will grow instead of your waistline!

Money Isn't the Problem

Your lack of fun isn't a problem of lifestyle. Don't blame it on the need to work, or your lack of money or leisure. You can't buy fun—or win or command it. Reaching your fondest goals won't secure it. Money and power don't help in the least. Neither do freedom, security, and unlimited time to play. That's why millionaires, movie stars, and celebrities aren't one bit happier than you are.

As a *Life Magazine* reporter I met and interviewed many of

the rich and famous: statesmen, actresses, geniuses and billionaires. And I found them beset with the same worry, anxiety, loneliness, and depression as the rest of us. They may have more time, toys, beauty, money, and power, but they don't have any more fun than you do. In fact, some of them have a good deal less. Their desperate hunger for fun is often what drove them to the top. Like you, they lost the ability to have fun when they were kids, and they haven't learned how to get it back.

We all yearn for fun. It's a universal craving, a fundamental need. You can easily test this for yourself. Simply ask your inner self, somewhere deep inside you, what you *really* want out of life, and why. Your first answers will probably be shallow and material—things like success, money, status and relationships. So go deeper and keep asking. Answer yourself honestly, peeling back the layers, descending to the depths of your desires. If you persist and you're truthful, you'll finally hit bedrock. You just want to have more fun. That's the bottom line.

Now ask yourself . . . Is there fun in my life or has it all been squeezed out, like the last of the toothpaste? When's the last time I really let go, letting fun take over? What do I do just for fun and for no other reason? Do I think of fun as a luxury? Am I getting as much fun out of life as I'd like? Or am I grimly working my way toward it? Is it somewhere up ahead, after I'm successful, once I have a little time? I hope!

This isn't a test, but the answers to these questions will hint at your level of fun. What should that level be? Well, if you go more than a few hours without having real fun, you're depriving yourself. Three times an hour is more like it! What must you do to find fun again? First, you have to recognize the value of fun. Then you have to recognize your need. When you've found the motivation, you have to give yourself permission to let fun back in your life. You have to *choose* fun.

That may mean changing some attitudes and beliefs about your right to have fun. You'll need to drop negative attitudes and self-destructive habits. You'll have to take responsibility for your life, instead of blaming it on "them" and accepting cruel fate and defeat. You'll need to take back the power you've given away to society (parents, teachers, employers, the church, and the state). You'll have to make up your mind to get serious about fun, and pursue it—now. Then you're ready to change your feelings and have fun full time—instead of accepting low-grade anxiety 90 percent of the time.

Once you've given yourself permission, you're ready for the hilarious techniques that teach you how to recapture fun and hold it again in your heart. Regaining your lost fun may not be easy at first, but it's simple and anyone can do it. Anyone! You don't have to be smart or educated. You don't need money, spare time or possessions. It doesn't cost a penny and you don't have to give up anything- -*except* your pessimism and gloom. Fun is free and available to everyone from peasant to president, from ogre to saint. It doesn't matter how long you've been fun-less, or even if you can't remember ever having any fun. All you need is desire.

Because fun is never lost, never dead, never beyond resuscitation. It's our birthright and it's patiently waiting to be discovered. We never lose our capacity for having fun. Our bodies are hungry for it, ready to let it in. Like seeds awaiting rain, we're ready to grow and bloom with fun. All you have to do is decide to change your feelings. In the pages that follow you'll learn how to let fun back into your life.

2

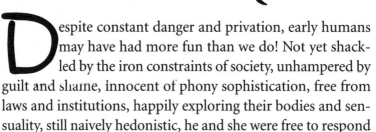

> "If a man insisted on always being serious and never allowed himself a bit of fun ... he would go mad."
> Herodotus, 425 BC

Whatever Happened to Fun?

(A Quick History)

Despite constant danger and privation, early humans may have had more fun than we do! Not yet shackled by the iron constraints of society, unhampered by guilt and shame, innocent of phony sophistication, free from laws and institutions, happily exploring their bodies and sensuality, still naively hedonistic, he and she were free to respond naturally to primal urges for fun and play without limitation from within or without.

Earliest man (and woman) probably found their first fun in sex. Unlike the animals they closely observed, they found they could couple anytime they wanted. And it felt wonderful! Uninhibited sex was an elemental source of dependably quick sharp pleasure.

Though they had to be constantly vigilant and alert (not yet living at the top of the food chain) they were curious, sensual, instinctive. The hope of coming pleasure, though crude by our standards, was reason enough to try and stay alive. "Pleasure," wrote anthropologist Lionel Tiger, "is vital to the preservation and survival of the species."

The Urge to Play

Though he had to be tough, distrusting, and focused on harsh reality, early man nonetheless must have noticed the playfulness of the young animals he stalked—and discovered a happy resonance in himself. Play produced a deep animal pleasure, well worth his imitation. As Sartre put it, "When man finds himself free, his preferred activity is play."

Sociologist Johan Huizinga found "an irreducible element of play in all the basic human cultural activities. Genuine pure play," he writes in *Man the Player*, "is one of the main bases of civilization. Play proceeds ... outside the sphere of necessity or material utility. The rules of mutual massacre closely mime those of play. War games employ the same rules as games whose purpose was rooted in pure pleasure."

Thorstein Veblen, in *The Theory of the Leisure Class*, says, "Economic competition is a game of ownership descended from the barbarian game of predatory war." Thus, the war we know as business was originally spawned by play.

In the earliest known societies, work and play were often combined, especially in religious festivals. Economically, play was an exchange of gifts. Since play was an integral part of early work, there was no division or conflict. In early civilization's stratified society, the leisure class ennobled play and pleasure. Historically, play was elevated by the upper classes to a full-fledged intellectual pursuit.

The lower classes in those early societies had to be satisfied with less structured and elaborate forms of fun and play. Because they hadn't the leisure of the elite, their fun, of necessity, was rough and ready, quick and dirty. ("I've taken my fun where I found it," wrote Kipling.) Because it had to be a part of daily life—and sometimes hidden from view—their fun was expressed in their attitude. And it was probably more genuine than the dilettante fun of their social superiors.

The civilizing effects of good manners and bathing later robbed us of the cruder forms of physical fun by arousing disgust at normal bodily functions. But down through the ages, fun has proven resilient. Despite pressure and disapproval, it always manages to survive, often surfacing in strange and peculiar ways—further evidence that it's essential to our happiness.

The early Greeks and Romans believed in pleasure, self-development, individual spontaneity and mental cultivation.

Aristotle taught that "All men seek happiness." Ovid advised, "While you can, have fun." Plato argued that life is a juxtaposition of pleasure and pain. Socrates warned that "It's not proper to cure the body without the soul." In the Bible, Ecclesiastes observes that "Gladness prolongs his days," and Proverbs declares "A merry heart doeth good like a medicine," and "A merry heart is the life of the flesh."

The earliest philosophers knew the value of fun. Their gods smiled to show approval, laughed to express pleasure. The sophisticated joys of life were assiduously pursued and artfully cultivated, especially by the privileged. But all classes sought fun more or less without restraint. Despite the hardships and uncertainties of primitive conditions, a look at world morality up through the fifteenth century reveals a leisurely and comfortable attitude toward life.

Our preindustrial ancestors know how to play. The human atmosphere at work and the comparatively easy pace encouraged fun. People enjoyed their work as well as their leisure. They laughed with their neighbors, played with their kids, savored sunsets and listened to the birds, enjoying the natural world. Regimentation was unknown.

The human need for fun and play was understood and respected. There was recognition of the right to moral freedom.

An orientation to social responsibility and individual welfare recognized human aspirations for fun and play in everyday life. Man lived outdoors and his life was in tune with the organic rhythms and sun time of the natural world. Business and the church had not yet grabbed control.

The Death of Fun

Then came the "Reformation" and the "Industrial Revolution," the fiercest enemies that fun has ever known. In sixteenth-century northern Europe, the comparatively liberal doctrines of the Roman Catholic Church were gradually replaced by the deeply repressive puritanism of the new protestantism. Embodying the Calvinist and Lutheran ethic of self-denial as moral purity, the reformists set their sights on destroying the free individualism of hedonistic fun and play that threatened their absolute control.

As chronicled in Max Weber's classic *The Protestant Work Ethic and the Spirit of Capitalism,* the old leisurely and comfortable attitude toward life gave way to a hard frugality, an anti social and immoral unlimited lust for gain that punished all who refused to adapt or conform. Monastic asceticism came out of the cells to view sloth as worse than covetousness, crushing all dissent. Diligence, sobriety, thrift, prudence, and piety were elevated to a position of unmixed virtue. Puritanism fit hand-in-glove with the Industrial Revolution, declaring the pursuit of wealth a sacred duty.

Capitalism became an orgy of naked materialism. Puritanism molded—and was molded by—the new social order. Commerce and the church conspired to control everyday life, producing a new repressive world morality, effectively driving traditional fun and play underground. Puritanism produced an unparalleled tyranny, an unbearable control of every individual under the watchful eye and terrible authority of the church. Asceticism came to dominate world morality.

In the 18th century, British Parliament, backed by the church, passed laws speeding up work production. At first, domestic workers protested against the unaccustomed regulation, but economic pressure forced them to knuckle under, and in time they came sadly to accept the new order.

With the loss of freedom came a decline in healthy sensuality and play. As work and puritanism gained dominion, people learned to postpone gratification, delay sensuality, forego spontaneity, disdain idleness, abandon their animal natures, and reluctantly forego their need for fun and play, even in leisure and private! Civilization dulled feelings as society imposed repressive rules. The body and mind underwent a split. Shame for natural functions developed, and sensual urges produced feelings of guilt.

In America, the inventor Benjamin Franklin typified early American puritanism, writing, "Time is money ... avoid all spontaneous enjoyment of life ... conform to capitalist rules ... be diligent in business ... earn all you can and give all you can to the church. The public welfare, the good of the many, is to be valued above our own."

By the 19th century, Western civilization had gone sour. Both Europe and America were thoroughly poisoned by the new social consciousness: "the greatest good for the greatest number." New educational aspirations came at the expense of individual freedom. Scientific judgement came to dominate society. By worshiping technological progress, we came to grotesquely over value economics.

Material interest, greed and gain, and a mania for improved living conditions lifted the GNP and sometimes the masses, but robbed the ordinary citizen of individuality, fun, and play. The church warned that sensual pleasure was suspect and quite possibly corrupting. It's ultimate pessimism was the insistence that "original sin" inescapably condemns all children to remain as unhappy, ignorant, and enslaved as their parents.

The Rise of Shame and Guilt

With the gradual shift in world morality, the new repressive values of the church filtered down into government, the schools, and finally to the heart and core of society, the family. Institutions of every kind jumped on the bandwagon to gang up on helpless fun, unwilling to miss a chance to bolster institutional authority and control. The state, the schools, and finally even parents joined the church in publicly condemning fun.

In sometimes subtle but devastating ways, fun was denigrated, scorned, ridiculed, made suspect, disdained and criticized as frivolous and childish by any and all in positions of authority, because fun's freedom and spontaneity threatened institutions of every kind. The sanitized fun that survived was often warped, joyless, perverted and impotent—but comparatively safe.

The rapacious pursuit of wealth reached its highest development under the free enterprise system in America, becoming an art form, attaining the character of sport. Max Weber called it "a naked greed devoid of all regard for social welfare." He saw early American puritanism to be empty of hedonism, opposed to the "joy of living," squeezing those who failed to conform. French philosopher Henri Bergson observed that "the ability to have fun and laugh at ourselves is ... notably absent in the narcissistic, immature U.S."

The elaborate, stylized, highly organized, ritualized games of the British aristocracy—cricket, billiards, bowls—are a parody of play from the people who gave us the "stiff upper lip" and ramrod-straight backbone while denying themselves any spontaneous expression of feeling. Asians save face in a different way. Japanese children are controlled by their parents and teachers by the dreaded threat of "being laughed at" by others.

The State of Fun Today

Truly, life hasn't been the same since the Reformation and Industrial Revolution destroyed the reputation of innocent fun, replacing it with shame, guilt, and institutional control. Old Ben Franklin would have been proud of society's strictures of the nineties: "Pay your dues," "Earn your way," "No pain, no gain."

We've paid a terrible price for the demise of fun. Since our fundamental need remains as strong as ever, the prohibition of fun by society makes us feel guilty and ashamed when we indulge our instinctive and continuing desires. It's a simple matter of cause and effect—elementary psychology. Instead of cherishing and enjoying fun and play, we've become tentative, doubtful, self-conscious, embarrassed, and insecure. We're afraid of what the neighbors might think. The disapproval of society makes us hesitate to play. Fear of embarrassment is so strong that one poll showed that death was often preferable to public embarrassment!

The barrier to fun hides invisibly in our minds. We block fun by means of a complicated system of screens and sensors. With the help of society's many narrow institutions (and our acceptance of them), we stop ourselves from having fun. It happens through the attitudes, assumptions, beliefs, feelings, expectations, and judgements we have built up over a lifetime. The stories we have learned and our perception of ourselves conspire to limit our fun. Lincoln said, "A man is as happy as his mind allows him to be."

We worry about what *might* happen and what we *should* do, dragged down by continuous vague anxieties. The shift in morals has undermined our resolve and erected a barrier to fun.

We've given away our power, accepted shame and guilt, and knuckled under to society's disapproval. We have phobias about fun, hangups over play.

"We live under a tyranny of *shoulds,*" wrote "psychologist Albert Ellis. He urged his patients to "Stop *should-ing* on yourself!" A case of the *shoulds* is rooted in low self esteem, guilt, and dependency on the opinion of others.

In this sad state, our relationships fail, we watch our neighbors to find out what's expected and socially acceptable, we can't seem to relax, society's greatest blandishments somehow fail to satisfy, and happiness always seems to elude us. We're frustrated, irritated, loveless, joyless and vaguely discontented. And we can't pinpoint why! The answer is simple: our minds and emotions have been poisoned by the "original sin" of fun, that disastrous sixteenth century shift in world morality. Puritanism was the cause; worry, guilt and shame are the result.

To compensate for our depressing gloom, in desperate search of lasting pleasure, we grow more permissive, hedonistic, sexually active, and attracted to stimulants and painkillers. But nothing seems to satisfy. Our frustration and neurosis lead to alcoholism, rage, and violence. Cut off from fun and play, we go for "fast, temporary relief," the familiar "quick fix," that leads in turn to emptiness, addiction, and burnout.

On the outside, society is free to the point of absurdity. On the inside, it's uptight, anxious and confused. We're still burdened by the shame and guilt spawned by puritanism, mentally and emotionally bogged down by the noxious Protestant work ethic. Western culture has failed to mature, and our society is stunted. We enjoy a level of personal liberty unknown elsewhere in the world, but it brings us no lasting pleasure. In our heads and hearts, we remain primitive, limited and adolescent, trapped between the heaven of ecstasy and the shame/guilt/worry of hell. We act and feel inept and neurotic, like petulant, spoiled, self-pitying children.

Caught between pleasure and guilt, we don't know how to live. The constant conflict leaves us frozen, unable to choose between our instinctive desire for fun and the mores of society. Technology has left us freer than ever before, but we're pathetically unable to translate our new toys and capabilities into pleasure. The schism has left us with a split personality. We're both freer and more repressed than other cultures. Science has supplanted religion as our guide. We rely on medical priests to tell us how to live. Industrialism and mechanization have robbed us of our pleasure ... and our leisure.

The Tyranny of Time

Perhaps the least known villain is "hurry up" time, the thief of modern life. Those in power impose impossible time restraints, claiming dire necessity, promising that our sacrifices will insure our security and survival. But just the opposite is true. Time is a whip beating constantly on all of us. We run faster and faster but never get where we're going. The speed-ed-up time world of the nineties is impatient, asocial, over-stimulating, unnatural, alienating, hard-driving—inhuman.

The clock has become our jailer. We count the days until weekends and holidays—and a chance for fun. But somehow there's never enough time. We retreat from the bogus beat of the culture to hide out in the gentle time of nature. Hurry-up time has squeezed the fun out of life—and the life out of us. But learning to have fun again can take us through the looking glass to slip the stress of accelerated time—and resurrect our ability to relax.

"Timewise," it's ironic that many so-called primitive societies are now far ahead of us. They still have time for recreation, freedom from restrictive work schedules, an interest in people, contact with the natural world, an outdoor life ordered by the slow beat of natural organic rhythms. The natives know how to have fun and relax, and they have the time to enjoy it. Having fun is important, and they live for the moment, unconcerned about the future. "Better to be happy than wise," is their motto. Of course, they don't spend seven hours a day watching television!

So we travel thousands of expensive miles to find fun and relaxation amid the smiling faces of the South Seas, the *mañana*-land of Mexico, the carefree monkeys of Africa—anywhere that's friendly, slow-moving, and easy-going. But our travels turn out to be fruitless. If we find what we want, it usually disappears as soon as we return.

Here at home, we're awash in the phony fun served up on the tube. The nineties have been declared "The decade of fun," because people are crying out for it, demanding it. And advertising agencies use that yearning to sell their products. But the phony fun they generate is only illusion and utterly fails to satisfy. Purely physical fun runs rampant in America, but real fun has never been so scarce.

New Hope for Fun

But the natives are growing restless. An insistent demand for real fun is piling up. People are rebelling against society's deprivations. Cultural control is slipping in the face of the onslaught. The dark ages are ending and a new day is dawning. We're beginning to witness the rebirth of fun.

Of course, it's been here all along, patiently waiting, within easy reach—if you're willing to make some fundamental changes in your attitude and outlook. The fun machine is ready and waiting. All you have to do to switch it on is change your feelings. Showing you how is what the rest of this book is about.

3

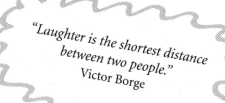

The Psychology of Fun

espite all the talk about it, fun is poorly understood. As badly as we want fun, we have a dangerous tendency to postpone it. We think we need ideal conditions—leisure, holidays, friends, romantic situations. We think we should "take time out" for fun. But waiting for fun doesn't work. You have to create it. The secret of full-time fun is to seek it in the worst situations. That's where you desperately need it. Finding fun in adversity can turn your life around. Waiting for ideal conditions is a trap ... because they never come.

Many people watch clowns and comedians to generate fun because they don't know how to create their own. They sit with frozen smiles on the edge of their seats, ready to go crazy at the first hint of amusement. They're starved for fun, but they've lost the capacity to produce their own. They have to have fun "done to them." Unfortunately, much of what comics deliver is based on ridicule, guilt, cheating, embarrassment, insult, sex, or toilet innuendo. It's forced, derogatory and utterly false.

When you learn to make your own fun, you won't have to go to clowns or comics for a fix. You'll find fun everywhere, and professional funmakers will seem a little sad instead of funny.

Another misconception involves the use of alcohol and drugs to "loosen up" and have a good time. Users of mood-altering substances are invariably seeking to inject a little fun into their lives. But they need help. Comics and funny movies aren't enough anymore, so they need something stronger. They use chemicals to replace pain with soothing, numbing, phony pleasure. They've lost the capacity for experiencing it for themselves without the crutch of chemical stimulation. But fun can miraculously change all that. Recapturing lost fun can help release dependency on alcohol and drugs. Fun can replace every kind of addiction!

In Other Words . . .

It may be helpful to precisely define a few commonly used but vaguely understood words. First come fun's companions, JOY and HAPPINESS. Happiness results from the deliberate satisfaction of basic needs, chiefly fundamental physical and emotional requirements, such as food, shelter and sexual gratification. Joy stems from the satisfaction of mostly mental and emotional needs. Insightful thinking, philosophizing, examination of principles, the deliberate pursuit of knowledge and improved understanding—all produce joy. Happiness and Joy, like fun, are related, overlapping aspects of pleasure.

Having defined the three aspects of pleasure, let's look at fun's three arch enemies, DIGNITY, DEVOTION, and DUTY. All three are dangerous because they're cloaked in virtue, drenched in uprightness, and rigorously employed by society to demolish dangerous fun.

Dignity is a trap, a snare, a delusion, the sworn enemy of fun. It's used by the church, the state, parents, and schools to maintain control and keep us chained to sobriety. Untold mis-

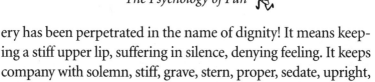

ery has been perpetrated in the name of dignity! It means keeping a stiff upper lip, suffering in silence, denying feeling. It keeps company with solemn, stiff, grave, stern, proper, sedate, upright, noble and sober. Dignity is a pretense, an unnatural stifling of human expression. It plays on feelings of guilt, shame, and embarrassment.

Devotion is the pious sister of dignity, a creation of the church. It means obedience and spiritual conformity, a uniformity of belief imposed by "higher" authority. Devotion means giving allegiance to a belief system devised by others, giving up independence and personal power, surrendering your right to question or rebel. It demands freedom-numbing self-denial.

Duty overlaps both dignity and devotion. "Devotion to duty" is a familiar, high-minded phrase used by pious righteous zealots to describe someone utterly selfless. But giving up the self is death. Selfless duty can produce all sorts of illness—especially cancer. It means submitting to others, toeing the line, practicing sheeplike obedience and lockstep conformity, and knuckling under to authority. It's emasculating and dehumanizing.

Of course, to have fun you needn't sacrifice all *natural* dignity, devotion, and duty ... providing they represent *your own personal feelings!* But beware! The three D's in any form are dangerous. They'll inhibit your fun if you don't watch out!

Embarrassment stems from giving validation of your life to others. Depend too much on the good opinion of other people and you're going to be embarrassed when you falter. For the insecure and powerless, failure must somehow be hidden, controlled, and suppressed in order to prevent embarrassment. They hide behind dignity, devotion and duty. Death, you'll recall, is often believed preferable to public embarrassment!

Play!

The ability to play is vital to finding fun because pure play *is* fun. By playfulness I mean frolicsome, antic, impish, lighthearted, heedless, high-spirited, mischievous, gay, frivolous, silly and spontaneous. The rediscovery of true playfulness is essential in recapturing our lost fun. Once we all possessed playfulness, but somehow it disappeared along with fun.

Pure playfulness is rare among adults, but fortunately it lives on in the very young. Children can teach us how to play . . . by example. Go to a children's park or playground and watch little kids playing. You'll see every kind of fun imaginable: pretending, yelling, running, fantasizing, jumping, making believe. You'll see kids unabashedly, unembarrassedly, unapologetically playing.

Kids know that fun and play live in your head. They're geniuses at play. It's what they do best because it's all they *want* to do. They live to play, they exist to have fun. If they're smart, they hold onto play for all they're worth.

Sadly, for most of us, play gets corrupted as we grow older. Suppressed anger and frustration turn into aggressiveness and hostility. Sexual impulses and a thirst for approval emerge to pollute pristine fun. A growing awareness of society and a sensitivity to its mores shift our values and make us look to others for validation. Play gets mean and competitive as we act out our various entrenched deprivations. Then other definitions of play take over: play your part, play jokes, play dumb, play for time, play possom, play around, play with fire, play the game, play to win.

The playfulness of youth turns into competition. Adult games are the opposite of playfulness, the enemies of fun. Competition rivals dignity, devotion and duty as a fun-killer — because it's rigorously taught to the impressionable young as a sterling unmixed virtue. ("We need to be more competitive," our leaders tell us.) Competitiveness is equated with success of every kind. It's the formula for getting ahead, getting your share—a euphemism for aggressive, ruthless, cutthroat, stop-at-nothing greed.

Psychologically, there are three reasons for competing: (1) to vent anger, tension, aggression and hostility; (2) to strive for peer approval by showing off and winning; (3) to enjoy fun-loving athleticism, exerting one's self for personal achievement, self measurement, physical pleasure, and companionship. Only number three qualifies as fun. There's enough inescapable competition in life without looking for more.

Worry, Anger, Anxiety, Guilt, etc.

There are several more highly subjective terms that need brief clarification.

WORRY is nothing more than anticipated anger. It's the number-one enemy of fun. Because we continually think and imagine, it's easy to think and imagine the worst. We imagine what *might* happen, concoct the very worst scenario, then convert it into reality. Our busy brains ask, "'what if' this disaster happens, 'what if' that calamity materializes?" We imagine how we'll feel if something "goes wrong." "If" somehow becomes "when," and when becomes certain and soon!

We grow angry at the wrongs we imagine, but we can't express the anger because the wrongs haven't actually happened. So we helplessly worry, stew, and agonize—effectively killing our chances of having fun. Worry is the arch-enemy of fun. The first step in combating it is understanding the process.

ANGER often masks half-hidden fear. Though widely viewed as negative, antisocial, sinful, poisonous, weak, and contemptible, anger (like fear) is merely an inescapable human emotion. There's nothing more satisfying, releasing, and delicious than the full appropriate expression of anger. Expressing it is healthy. Suppressing or denying it is dangerously destructive. Unexpressed anger will poison you, destroy your health, and ultimately it will kill you. It may not say so in the coroner's reports, but millions of people die every year of bottled up, repressed anger—called heart disease and cancer. Nothing is more self-destructive.

Just as anger leads to worry and ill health, it figures in the definitions of guilt and depression.

GUILT is anger you don't feel you have a right to express. You think you don't deserve to express it. It's your cross, your burden, something you have to bear and endure. (Not true. Just forgive yourself, and forget it.)

DEPRESSION is anger you worry about, pain you anticipate, anger that would get you into trouble if you dared to express it. Since you feel you can't escape it, you slide into depression—now classified as the "common cold" of mental illness. Depressing!

FEAR is merely anticipated loss or failure. It's the expectation that you won't be able to handle some specific situation. When you're afraid, you don't believe you can cope. (The antidote to fear is simply self-trust. To defeat its limitations, you have to build the belief that you can handle whatever comes your way.)

HURT is a wound, an emotional laceration, sometimes a spiritual loss. Hurts take time to heal; healing doesn't happen overnight.

ANXIETY is a vague mix of anger, hurt, self-pity, doubt, confusion and fear. It's distinct from fear in that you can't quite unscramble it or pinpoint its cause.

With these often misunderstood words clarified, at least for our purposes, we can talk more precisely about changing feelings to resurrect fun.

4

"The art of medicine consists of amusing the patient while nature cures the disease."
Voltaire

What the Experts Say ...

Modern science increasingly confirms what wise men have known for centuries: that having fun is the key to happiness and health. Sages, philosophers, and holy men through the ages have venerated and prescribed fun for every ailment of the body, heart, and soul. Now psychologists, sociologists, anthropologists, health surveyors, medical researchers, and shrinks of every stripe are rediscovering fun's virtues.

Study after study points to fun's role in increased longevity, creativity, and productivity, better health, sex, sleep, and improved relationships.

Diverse research, conducted for other purposes, often ends up concluding that fun and play are tremendous tools for lifting mankind, essential to our well-being, curative, and vital to health and happiness. Optimistic beliefs and positive expectations lead to success, happiness, and fun. Fun improves health—and optimism produces fun. It's a delightful circle.

Robert Ornstein, Ph.D., and David Sobel, M.D., in their 1991 book *Healthy Pleasures,* present convincing evidence. "Hun-

dreds of scientific studies on thousands of people," they write, "report that individuals who expect the best, are hopeful, optimistic, and enjoy sensual pleasures ... are, in general, healthier and live longer," while "negative moods, depression, hostility and ... lack of pleasure ... seem to contribute to poor health."

For instance, a study of 2000 Chicago Western Electric Co. workers over two decades showed that depressed workers were twice as likely to die of cancer, suffer heart attacks, and require bypass surgery than happier patients. Depression in one study was a better predictor of future heart problems than artery damage, high cholesterol and cigarette smoking.

Single, separated, divorced or widowed people were two to three times more likely to die prematurely than were their married peers—and five to ten times more likely to be hospitalized for mental disorders. Heart disease, cancer, tuberculosis, arthritis, and pregnancy problems all increase in likelihood with weakened social connectedness. So learning to have fun (a dependable cure for depression) will help make you healthier. "When I'm happy, I'm never sick," claimed French philosopher Rene Dubois. "I only become sick when I'm unhappy."

There is dramatic research evidence that changing negative feelings bolsters the immune system. We can actually boost our immunity by lifting our mood. If you're "up" you're healthier and less likely to get sick than when you're "down." A study showed that patients laughing at the antics of comedian Richard Pryor enjoyed higher immune function while they were laughing. You're healthier while you're having fun.

Studies show consistently that optimists recover quicker, stay healthier, live longer, and enjoy life more. Since optimism is essential to both health and fun, it's probably the most valuable quality you can cultivate. (You'll learn how in the next chapter.) The bedrock upon which optimism rests is "positive expectation," the happy belief that life is and will be good. Few adults are blessed with unbridled optimism, but it can easily be learned. Scientific research has shown repeatedly that changing negative feelings, building positive expectation, and developing optimism miraculously restore the ability to have fun —while producing improved health.

The "placebo effect" proves that positive expectation works. Placebos are make-believe medicines without medicinal value that are seriously prescribed to give the patient the expectation of curative benefits. The intent is to help the patient, not to deceive him. Dozens of studies over the years have conclusively shown that an average 40 percent of patients routinely show substantial improvement after taking pretend medicine that they believe will confer benefits.

Placebos can be more effective than the most powerful drugs because it's the positive expectation, not the medicine, that is curative! Science says the positive expectation (the placebo effect) stimulates the body's production of endorphins (pain relievers) in the brain, bringing about recuperation. This positive suggestion has been used to clot the blood in hemophiliacs, cure skin diseases, remove warts, even enlarge women's breasts. So the first rule of cure is to BELIEVE you'll be cured.

Positive expectations can therefore be powerful healers. Conversely, negative expectations can make you sick or even kill you. Optimists are nourished by positive expectations, producing positive moods, which, like fun, bring success and good health. They focus on the good things, so that's what they get. A whole series of studies showed people whose expectations were high enjoyed far better health than the people who didn't.

In a study of cardiac surgery patients, optimists' lungs functioned better and they made speedier recoveries than did pessimists. A fun-seeking attitude fosters the needed optimism. There's plenty of evidence that fun makes us feel better and live longer, healthier lives, because we resist breakdown and

disease. Having fun turns on the body's powerful ability to heal and maintain health.

Studies also show that happiness depends more on how much of the time a person spends feeling good, rather than on momentary peaks of ecstasy. It's "how often," not "how much." A life filled with frequent small pleasures will be far happier than one with only a few giant successes.

Our mood swings vary with our expectations. What we imagine and expect is what we get. We take on the mood generated by our expectations. We behave according to our present feelings. So, to maximize our success, we need to keep ourselves in a happy frame of mind.

Healthy people expect to be healthy. When it comes to health, and most other things, healthy people are confirmed optimists. Modern psychological and clinical research has concluded that healthy people, expecting to be pleased, create a whole set of positive illusions.

Why illusions? Because the illusion of reality is all we really have. Our view of life is extremely limited. We each live in our own little world, each seeing only our own narrow slice of life. Our viewpoint reflects what we already believe. And what we believe is our interpretation of what we experience.

Studies show that healthy, hardy, happy people (optimists) believe in their ability to control their own destiny. They believe themselves likable and important. They minimize the importance of setbacks and expect to succeed. They focus their attention on the good things that happen to them, denying the importance of negative events. They believe in a bright future, expecting success. They're happy and find fun all around them.

Healthy people remember their past successes and good times, and they expect more of them in the present and future. Anticipation of a rosy future is a joy in itself, and it leads, the experts claim, to success of every kind. The optimistic outlook benefits us twice — in the present pleasure of anticipation and the increased likelihood of future success. Happy people know how to use healthy positive denial to reinforce optimism.

In a study of patients facing gallbladder surgery, the group that denied the threatening aspects of the surgery experienced fewer complications and required less pain medication than the group that had worried about the risks and dangers of the operation beforehand. By denying the apparent reality of the situation, the optimists "got through" the crisis better than the pessimists who "prepared" for it.

A group of patients facing open heart surgery were tested beforehand to determine their attitudes toward it. Those who expressed confidence in the outcome — and optimism and trust in their surgeons — recovered more quickly and showed a lower death rate than those with "normal" or pessimistic attitudes. It was the same with women about to undergo biopsies for cervical cancer. Three-quarters of the time, the more hopeful the patient, the less likely she was to have cervical cancer.

We all fear helplessness and loss of control over our lives, but beliefs vary in depth. Researchers found that people who believed they had control showed far less stress. Patients who were told they would be able to control blood loss during spinal surgery lost an average of only 500 ccs of blood, compared to 900 ccs in the control group. Optimists tend to believe they are in control and able to make changes and create success.

In a study of arthritis patients, those who had a positive attitude and felt a sense of control improved, while those who felt helpless didn't. Expectations of future health, studies show, have more effect on the end result than all the diets, stress relief schemes, and exercise plans combined!

During a seven-year study of 3500 senior citizens in Canada, those who rated their health as "poor" were almost three times as likely to die as those who claimed their health was

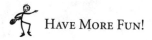

"good." Their optimism turned out to be even more powerful than the predictions of their doctors! Pessimistic patients rated as healthy by their doctors died more often than optimistic patients who had been diagnosed as unhealthy! The only thing that counted was what they themselves believed.

In another study, elderly people listed all the positive things they had to look forward to, classifying themselves as optimists or pessimists. Two years later, the optimists were decidedly healthier than the pessimists. They reported fewer colds, felt less tension, had more energy, and missed less work.

It was the same with patients facing coronary bypass. Those with optimistic outlooks showed fewer complications and recovered more quickly than the others. When AT&T went through a giant reorganization, the optimistic executives who believed they were in control of their lives experienced half the stress and health problems of those who felt helpless, threatened, and powerless in the face of uncertainty. Point of view made the difference.

Most of us don't think of ourselves as pessimistic—just accurate, realistic, and intelligently cautious. But that isn't optimism! The way we explain events often reveals a dangerous latent negativity. College students in one study revealed enough pessimism in the way they told their stories to accurately predict more sick days and visits to the doctor. In another study, thirty years after returning from World War II, optimistic veterans were far healthier than pessimists. In still another, baseball stars confident of their ability lived longer than those who modestly explained their past success as mere luck.

Patients with advanced breast and skin cancers who were joyful and optimistic stayed symptom free longer after treatment than did others. If cancer is marginal or an illness is just beginning, your attitude can be critical to your future. Comparisons of blood samples showed that the substantially higher white cell count of optimists successfully defended against tumor formation. Optimists passionately believe they will succeed. They are confident of their abilities. They live longer, happier, healthier lives—because they expect to!

What do all these studies of the positive effects of optimism on health have to do with having fun? They demonstrate that attitude is everything. And attitudes can be changed. We're not helpless victims of chance, luck, or fate. The power is within us to to find true success, no matter how bad things may presently look—and that includes finding fun. We can change our feelings, our attitudes, and beliefs to get what we really want: more fun out of life.

Still more studies show that our feelings, thoughts,and attitudes are major contributors to our physical well being and our ability to recover from illness. Conversely, unchecked daily stress causes and perpetuates illness. Angry men were found to be dependably more prone to heart attack. Thus, fun is both preventative and curative.

Dr. William Fry, Jr. found that laughter exercises the whole cardiovascular system. During hearty laughter, blood pressure rose, then fell; lungs were vigorously oxygenated, muscles released tension, natural opiates flooded into the brain to create well-being and pain relief. Twenty seconds of hearty laughter, it was found, has the beneficial effect of three minutes of hard aerobic exercise.

A study of students showed that changes in facial expression can trigger mood changes. Students consistently remembered happier thoughts when they were smiling. So a smile, even if it's forced, can lift gloom. By starting with a smile, you prime the pump for fun. And when we smile we turn our focus away from pain. Dr. David Bresler of the UCLA Pain Control Unit not only encourages his patients to fight pain by smiling, he writes them prescriptions to go to the mirror and smile twice each hour.

Smiling and laughter are both contagious. By smiling you disarm your opponent, thus gaining an advantage. Robbers of convenience stores testified in court that they never bothered storekeepers who greeted them with a smile! Even looking at a smiling face confers benefits, says Dr. John Diamond. It provides the viewer with positive energy. And smiling strengthens the thymus gland, a vital contributor to our immune systems.

Benefits of Play

A 1978 study of 231 Polish television viewers found that play strengthened social integration and satisfied needs for both fantasy and new experience. For 70 percent, play was escape from everyday routine; for 35 percent, it allowed work to be forgotten; for 18 percent, it alleviated tension and produced energy; another 18 percent found it counteracted social isolation; and 28 percent said play produced pure joy and new experience.

A 1981 study found that volunteers had more fun and were more playful on the job than paid workers, due to lessened job responsibility and a more permissive attitude. A 1975 German study found that the three prerequisites for play in animals were (1) a rich and varied relationship with the environment, (2) freedom from struggle for food and shelter, and (3) genuine security in the group and environment.

A 1977 study found that play in the minds of many people was actually opposed to reality. Play and the world of play were found to be extremely fragile. The German study of animals suggests why, and it offers hints for learning how to play and have fun again.

Brain studies show that disease is linked to beliefs about oneself. The most important aspect of healing comes from within. Placebo effect provides the proof. It's been proven effective in every kind of therapeutic procedure. And patients optimistic about the effects of surgery enjoyed fewer complications, quicker healing, less anxiety, bleeding, pain, and depression. The patient's emotional state, mood, will to live, and belief in his doctor are therefore more important than all the medicines he takes! Optimistic physicians who prescribe enthusiastically greatly improve their patient's results!

Studies show that the message delivered with the treatment determines how rapidly it will take effect. Beliefs conveyed by doctors are converted into the beliefs of the patient. Ironically, the more unpleasant the treatment, the easier it is to believe in, studies show. Familiar brand names and high prices help convince the innocent patient of what he wants to believe. As Norman Cousins observed, "The placebo is not so much a pill as a process. It works because the human body is its own best apothecary."

In a famous study of the 1950s, some 10,000 operations were performed to relieve chest pain from heart disease by tying arteries. But some of the doctors, skeptical of the procedure's benefits, decided to conduct an experiment. They opened up every patient but secretly tied the arteries of only half of them! Because they believed they had received the full treatment, these "untied" patients enjoyed just as much physical benefit as those who'd had their arteries tied!

Thirty-two women were told in twelve weekly sessions that their breasts would enlarge as a result of a harmless weekly (placebo) treatment. Because they came to believe in the treatment, 85 percent enjoyed some breast enlargement, and 46 percent required a larger bra size. Thoughts and beliefs were similarly used to control skin eruptions from poison oak, bleeding after tooth extraction, and inflammation and blistering from burns.

Another study showed that fun is catching. People closeted with a euphoric person felt their mood and spirits lift. Elderly people with the company and support of spouses or friends were found to be far less likely to commit suicide. Beliefs control a far greater part of our actions than most of us recognize. A small shift in our perceptions can make the difference between hope and despair. Every known system of medicine works through our beliefs.

The best predictor of improvement of arthritis symptoms was how likely the patient thought he or she would improve. One of the best predictors of future health is the patient's own expectations.

Albert Schweitzer, speaking of African medicine, explained, "The witch doctor succeeds for the same reason all of us succeed. Each patient carries his own doctor inside him."

The biggest factor in longevity, a seven-year study showed, is social contact. Married people who had fun with friends had twice the life expectancy of singles—no matter what else they did.

"Happiness is part of the fight for recovery from cancer," says Harold Benjamin. His Santa Monica Wellness Community helps patients fight cancer through laughter. Laughter, it's been found, reduces the levels of certain hormones that are generated by stress. It also increases the activity of killer cells that attack tumors. Benjamin's patients put great vigor into jokefests, happy visualization, and social networking because they know their lives may depend on it. Many a patient has laughed his way back to health.

"Ten minutes of genuine belly laughter had an anesthetic effect that would give me at least two hours of pain-free sleep," wrote Norman Cousins.

Cousins knew how to generate his own fun by playing jokes on hospital nurses. Once, he secretly filled a urine specimen bottle with apple cider from his lunch tray. When the nurse came to collect it she observed that it looked a little dark.

Cousins held it up to the light. "By George, you're right," he said. "Lets run it through again." Whereupon he uncorked it and drank it down with relish, enjoying the shocked expression of the disbelieving nurse.

Caring for others also increases life expectancy. Responding to a cry for help warms our hearts and brings deep satisfaction. A study found that humans are genetically disposed to helping fellow creatures. It's a primal instinct and provides a fundamental pleasure which stimulates health and longevity more than any other factor. Generosity feels good because giving is close to loving, and loving (not receiving love) is the greatest source of human happiness.

Confiding childhood terrors and traumas, a study showed, reduces the chance of developing hypertension, ulcers, and cancer, as well as colds and flus. By bringing hidden fears out into the light, we defuse them and lessen their influence on our lives. We break the endless loop of negative thoughts and feelings that fuel constant worry and vague anxieties. Failure to express feelings, experts increasingly agree, leads to cancer. When you internalize feelings—choke them down, suppress or repress them—you're poisoning yourself as surely as if you take a little arsenic each time you get mad but don't let the anger show.

How we think literally determines our state of health. Studies show that optimists catch fewer infectious diseases, enjoy better health, live longer and have stronger immune systems. The key to finding fun is . . . *expecting* it. "Seek and ye shall find." Spontaneous, childish, impulsive people are more apt to be happy and healthy. Today's experts have joined wise men throughout history in confirming the value of life-renewing fun and play.

5

> During the dark days of the war, President Abe Lincoln often read to his cabinet from a joke book, cracking up at every punchline. When the cabinet sat stonefaced, he asked, "Gentlemen, why don't you laugh? If I couldn't laugh I should die!"

Get Ready for Fun!

To give yourself a jump start down the yellow brick road to fun, you need to make finding fun top priority—more important than anything else, your bottom line goal. That means putting yourself first, being a little selfish. Beware the trap of postponing fun or making yourself earn it. Don't copy society by making it conditional on achievement.

And make up your mind to live in the present, focusing on the now, resolving to squeeze every possible drop of pleasure from each moment. Nothing kills fun like reliving past failures and worrying about the future. Forget the past and build a bright future by deciding to maximize fun in the present.

Before you're ready for big-time fun. it may be necessary to demolish a few major barriers—like pessimism, negative beliefs, lack of self-esteem, dependency on others, limited expectations, lingering anxieties, and destructive old habits. Worry, constant comparison with others, and embarrassment may also block fun by making you feel foolish, hesitant, tentative, or uncertain.

Maybe part of you still thinks that responsible adults aren't supposed to have fun, that it's undignified, "kid stuff." Or you're ashamed of wanting to play. Perhaps life has been hard and you've been deprived of fun a long time. Maybe you didn't get much as a kid.

Whatever the reason, to release the brakes you probably need to change some attitudes, feelings, and beliefs. You may need to give yourself permission to have fun again, to allow fun back into your life. That's what this chapter is about—providing a bridge between the universal yearning for fun and your ability to experience it fully for yourself.

Man is the only animal that laughs—because he thinks and imagines. Man, the laugher, alas, is also man the worrier. Sadly, his greatest strengths can become his greatest weaknesses. The thinking and imagining that bring fun and laughter make him vulnerable to worry, susceptible to anxiety. But science tells us that man has tremendous untapped potential. His great mental capacity allows him to learn and change—to reach for fun while overcoming worry and anxiety—by using his little known ability to change his feelings.

Changing Feelings

Almost from page one, I've insisted that changing feelings is the key to finding fun. Now it's time to try it. Most people never dream of trying to change their feelings. They go through life locked into certain habitual reactions, even though they hate them. To some people, the idea of changing feelings will be shocking and revolutionary—maybe even threatening. Others will find it a revelation. They'll see the exciting potential for escaping negativity and increasing happiness.

If you don't like your feelings, change them! It sounds simple, and it is—even if it isn't always easy. Your feelings belong to you alone. They aren't carved in stone or set in concrete. You're in control . . . or should be. You don't have to react in ways you don't like. You're free to laugh instead of cry, be optimistic instead of pessimistic, smile instead of worry.

Don't blame other people for the way they make you feel. "They" can't touch your feelings. Only you can do that. The fact is, you choose all your feelings. Unfortunately, you usually do it by default. You let yourself emotionally react automatically. How you react is determined by your lifetime accumulation of beliefs and expectations, many of them hurtful or negative. But you don't have to react habitually. If you don't like your usual knee-jerk reactions, decide to consciously change them! All it takes is the decision to react the way you want—a way that makes you happy. *Happiness is a Choice.* That's the title of a Ballantine book by Barry Kaufman. And it's true.

Wouldn't you like to set yourself free? Change your feelings and you change your life! It's up to you. Changing negative feelings is the key to finding fun. So give it a try. You've nothing to lose but the negative feelings you don't like.

By "feelings" I mean your customary emotional response to a particular situation. Feelings stem from our beliefs, which in turn derive from our interpretation of a lifetime of experience. You can't change that experience, but you *can* change your interpretation of it. You can change your feelings simply by deciding to change your beliefs about any given situation. You're free to discard your old reactions to escape the unwanted feelings they produce.

Many old interpretations, made when we were kids, no longer accurately represent our adult knowledge and understanding. But often it doesn't occur to us to update them and thus get rid of inaccurate, outdated, unpleasant feelings. We say, "That really bugs me," or "I hate it when someone..." or "I can't help how I feel." We go through life locked into feelings we don't like, missing out on fun, reacting unconsciously—never realizing that we have within us the power to change any feeling.

For example, maybe you feel resentful, angry, righteous, even outraged when you encounter conceit—someone putting on airs. If you don't like those draining feelings, ask yourself, do I *have* to feel this way? Does her conceit really hurt me? How would I rather feel? Couldn't I be amused? Or not react at all? Or turn my attention elsewhere—looking instead for fun? Or laugh at myself for caring how she acts?

During my years in Primal Therapy, my new-found feelings were sacred and precious to me. I'd gone through a lot to unearth and learn to express them. Unfortunately, many of them were negative and unpleasant. Then I discovered Feeling Therapy, in which I learned to change my feelings from bad to good. That profound discovery changed my life, allowing me to integrate the many gains I had made in Primal into a much happier daily life. Once I realized that I had a choice, changing my feelings became largely a matter of developing awareness—and acting upon it.

The concept was so great that it was hard, at first, to believe that changing feelings didn't have any down side. It seemed too good to be true, like changing lead into gold. But after twenty years, all I've lost is a lot of unwanted negativity. Now you can learn to change your feelings a lot quicker and easier than I did by learning from my distilled experience.

Here's the sequence of events:

1. Change begins with dissatisfaction with your current feelings.

2. Next comes an ardent desire for change and a resolve to try.

3. The knowledge that you *can* change any feeling helps release the grip of negativity. Understanding that you aren't stuck with bad feelings forever—unless you want to be—is liberating.

4. Examine a particular reaction you want to change, searching for the underlying beliefs that produce it.

5. Then, demolish those beliefs by replacing them with the positive, optimistic ones you prefer.

6. Or simply skip steps 4 and 5 and jump straight from the bad feelings that drag you down to the ones that make you feel good.

The rest of this chapter deals with myriad strategies and techniques for changing those lead-like feelings into gold, in order to find fun and feel good.

Identify Your Beliefs

We're often unaware that we constantly talk to ourselves— rehearsing our private stories, worrying, taking our emotional temperatures, worrying, examining our feelings, worrying. We never stop talking, but we don't really listen to what we say—not objectively. Our stories become habitual, set in concrete. We don't question their validity, so they become our beliefs. This small talk controls our moods, decisions, and activities of every kind—in fact the whole direction of our lives. We act on these haphazard beliefs as though they were gospel, and we think we're being logical and objective!

But all this limited and negative perception drastically limits our health, happiness, and success of every kind. Fortunately, we can change our stories and beliefs—and we must if we want to succeed and have fun. The first step in changing is to listen objectively and become aware of our actual attitudes and beliefs. So find a quiet distraction-free time and place, and concentrate on the perpetual inner dialogue, being sensitive to the way it makes you feel. Pay attention to your stories and be ready to pick them apart.

As you listen to what you tell yourself, ask some pointed

questions. Do you like what you are hearing? Is it optimistic, open, helpful, happy, unlimited? Or is it narrow, doubtful, critical, and anxious? Try to spot the silly limitations and illogical assumptions. Look in the cobwebby corners of your mind at the many ways you scare yourself and hold yourself back. Ask questions that will reveal your feelings, motives, fears, attitudes, and beliefs, to uncover the ways you are blocking out fun.

Ask, for instance, Do I hold rigid, black and white views? Do I make blind and unwarranted assumptions? Do I frequently use the words "always" and "never?" Do I look for worst-case scenarios? Do I use negative "what ifs" to restrict my action? Do I routinely expect the worst? Do I demand perfection? Do I blame myself or others for what goes wrong? Do I look for alternative solutions? Do I expect small failures to be permanent and catastrophic?

If you don't like what you hear, reconsider your habitual beliefs. Do they fit your current desires or are they sadly out of date? Will they lead you to success, happiness, health, and fun? It's time to root out the hidden pessimism masquerading as realism, the self-protection and survival and defense against hurt feelings and embarrassment. See how limited you've been, how critical, denying, blaming, dependent on others—and fearful of change.

Unearth the traumas of youth that led you down a negative path. By bringing them out in the light of day, you defuse them, distance them, and lessen their influence on your life. You break the endless cycle of negative thought and feeling, opening the way to positive change. The time you spend listening objectively to yourself, becoming aware and determining to change, can turn your life around, leading you to the fun you want and deserve.

So target things that bother you. Isolate some of your more ridiculous stories, habits, and insupportable beliefs. Write down each discovery with the resolve to change it, to make it compatible with the kind of life you want. Carry reminders—3 x 5 cards, a string tied on one finger, or a rubber band around your wrist—to help you stay aware. Look for connections between a particular adversity and the feelings and beliefs it generates. Try to separate your thoughts from your feelings. Remember, feelings are results, not causes. The thoughts came first, creating the beliefs that determine your feelings. You have to isolate your negative beliefs before you can begin to change them.

Here's a four-step procedure to help you classify and evaluate your most persistent problems and anxieties.

1. Demand evidence that what you're saying to yourself is unassailably accurate. Hunt for underlying negative beliefs. Pounce on inaccuracies. Search for flaws like a tough prosecutor destroying a weak defense witness.

2. Look for alternative (more optimistic) explanations. Try to see the problem as temporary, limited, and impersonal—and thus less threatening.

3. Soberly check the odds of this catastrophe actually occurring. See how crazy and preposterous your anxieties really are.

4. Question the value of your negative beliefs. Will they help you? Do they lead to fun? Or do they sabotage and delay success?

If you can't rout those negative beliefs on your own, get a mate or trusted friend to help you. You need someone with whom you can share intimate feelings without covering up or getting defensive. Confide the negative beliefs you have unearthed and get your pal to attack them with the above four weapons, setting them up for you to finish off.

Banishing Pessimism

Habitual pessimism is a fun-killer, while an optimistic outlook opens the door and lets fun in. Fun seekers can't overdo optimism. There's no such thing as too much. Optimism brings you the courage, spirit, confidence, opportunity and frame of mind needed to let go and have fun. Martin E. P. Seligman, in his book *Learned Optimism,* offers us precise definitions. The pessimist views trouble as doom. He sees it as permanent, hopeless, inescapable, and all his fault.

The optimist sees trouble as temporary, limited, and nothing to do with him. Whatever the event, he confidently says, "If it's bad, its not my fault, and it will soon pass away and never come again. If it's good, I'll take the credit. It's going to last forever and it will help me a lot." He cheerfully believes in having things both ways. He doesn't care a fig about being inconsistent. Using positive denial, he stubbornly expects the best, no matter what. He sees the world through rose-colored glasses.

To figure out whether you're more an optimist or pessimist, take this test. Ask yourself, "When I fail, how do I feel? What do I think? How do I act?" The pessimist feels, thinks, and expects helplessness, so that's how he acts. The optimist sees hope, help, and a rosy future, so he is energized. Optimism cures depression, leads to achievement, good health, well-being, and the positive expectation and pleasant state of mind that are the very foundation of fun.

If you're less than optimistic, there are two basic strategies for changing your outlook: (1) "Bandaid," passive, mechanical distractive techniques, and (2) the aggressive, permanent, more effective antidote of active disputation and positive denial.

DISTRACTION means doing something decisive to divert yourself when you find you're feeling, thinking, or acting pessimistic. For instance, you can slap the nearest wall hard and yell,

"Stop!" Or stamp your feet violently. Or wear a rubber band around your wrist, giving it a loud stinging snap to divert you from unwanted gloom. Or have pre-packaged happy thoughts waiting, and make a determined switch when pessimism strikes. Or you can promise to give your negativity full consideration—later—as an excuse for dropping it right now, thus robbing it of its immediate impact, urgency, and purpose.

Vastly more effective than distraction for getting rid of negative thought is actively rebelling against it. Once you recognize the culprit, you vehemently deny, dispute, reject, dismiss, let go, protest, and challenge your gloom.

POSITIVE DENIAL and DISPUTATION are the chief tools in the eradication of unwanted, negative, limited, and unhappy beliefs. Denial is defined as "the mental operation by which thoughts, feelings, acts, threats, or demands are minimized or negated." Pessimists have always taught us that denial is dangerous. They fatalistically caution us to "face reality," "take responsibility," "get in touch with feelings" and "be honest." But positive denial is healthy and beneficial. Optimists depend upon it. Flexibility of mind is the key to the healthy use of denial.

Remember, it isn't adversity that strikes you down, it's your negative beliefs about it. So batter those negative beliefs objectively and unmercifully. Protest vehemently against them. Argue for a more optimistic explanation of your feelings, one that won't drag you down. When you manage to let go you'll feel a wonderful surge of relief. You'll be energized, uplifted, and ready for unlimited fun. There's no bigger transformation you can make than changing from pessimism to an optimistic outlook.

Restoring Self Esteem

Low self-esteem has been shown by psychologists to block fun by withholding permission. You have to feel worthy to

allow fun into your life. Lack of self-esteem is also tightly tied to another of fun's enemies: Dependency on the Good Opinion of Others. If you worry about appearances or what the neighbors think, you're a victim of Outside Validation. You let others—society or some segment of it—dictate your values. You've given away your power, surrendered your identity and individual sovereignty.

Shrinks claim we all look full time for more self-esteem, but most of us look in the wrong place. The same society that took away our fun has taught us to seek self-esteem in the good opinion of others, with disastrous results. Outside validation has proved to be addicting, crippling, and obsessive. It creates inevitable no-win competition and steals our personal power, breeding dependency. It yields dependable resentment, a drive for unattainable perfection, a low level of trust and a high level of guilt.

The true source of self-esteem is *internal* validation. You build it six ways.

1. Be honest. Always tell the truth—especially to yourself. Listen to your feelings and act on them. They're a dependable index of your honesty. Honesty always feels good.

2. Be responsible. Act or react appropriately as an adult.

3. Display integrity, which merely means acting honestly and responsibly—right now. Real integrity is automatic and spontaneous. You don't have to think about it.

4. Trust yourself. Be willing to risk acting on what you believe. Don't let worry stop you. Act in spite of your fears.

5. Follow your deepest feelings. Listen to your heart, trust it, and act accordingly. Let your inner emotions be your guide.

6. Don't consciously hurt others either mentally or emotionally. Deliberately hurting others kills self-esteem.

Follow these six guidelines and you'll build true self-esteem and at the same time get rid of destructive outside validation. You'll be knocking down two roadblocks at once, paving the way for permission to have fun again. It can be difficult to juggle all six at once, so concentrate on just one or two each day.

A Gallup survey showed that people with respectable self-esteem were more easily able to make big changes in their lives because they already felt good about themselves—and wanted to feel even better. So self-esteem is a primary pipeline to fun and success.

And building self-esteem may be easier than you think. The same study showed that the odds for successful change are surprisingly good. If you take a shot at change, you're highly likely to land on your feet. Most people find it's easier than expected.

You Are What You Believe

A major seven-year study showed that belief/expectation goes a long way toward determining reality. If you believe in the power of fun, it can transform you. If you expect to have fun, you will. That's why optimists succeed while pessimists fail. They both expect to. How can optimistic belief open the door to fun? By destroying the barrier of negative expectancy.

Changing expectancy and reversing beliefs needn't be mind-wrenching. You already know how to do it—on a small safe scale. When you settle down to read a story or watch a movie, you "willingly suspend disbelief." You open up and risk believing for the sake of entertainment. You take a chance on experiencing the feelings that believing may produce.

A "willing suspension of disbelief" can get you over the

hurdles that block fun from your life. Just apply it to your life. Start small and work up. Begin with relatively safe events, then get progressively braver. Try to emulate the open, trusting outlook of a child. Make up your mind to banish cynicism. Look at the world through more trusting eyes. Don't pre-judge people or events. Open to undreamed of possibilities.

Another strategy is to stop babying yourself! Decide you're *going* to change—NOW! Cold turkey! Get tough with yourself—disgusted by your timid procrastination. Take a hard look at lingering old habits that limit you, and say "ENOUGH!" Take a chance. Throw caution to the winds and just DO it. Let newly-learned optimism and heightened self- esteem lift you over the hurdles.

Remember, *we are what we believe.* We will get what we expect. Reality is nothing more than a combination of our desires, imagination, and expectancy. So we need to focus first on our desires—what we really want. Just wanting to have fun will increasingly make it happen. We can also help ourselves by making an effort to be spontaneous, to follow our hearts and make way for play. So, be open to spur-of-the-moment, impromptu opportunities for fun. They can melt rigidity, shake up your habits, put flexibility in your routine, and add sparkle to your life. Slow down, loosen up, relax and have fun.

Actions don't dictate our feelings, we do—according to our habits, beliefs and attitudes. The choice is ours. We can passively let old habits bring us unwanted negative reactions, or we can actively change to feelings that make us happier. It's up to us. So make up your mind to react the way you want, not according to old habit.

Attacking Worry

Worry," you'll recall, is nothing more than anticipated anger, a helpless belief that future events will somehow bring defeat. If you're a worrier, the first step toward change is to listen to your inner monologue objectively, to find out exactly what you're telling yourself, to identify the enemy. Then resolve to fight back with everything you've got. Here's my arsenal of weapons for attacking worry, to clear the decks for unlimited fun.

First there's SIX STEPS:

1. Isolate and delineate the specific problem that's bugging you.

2. Verbally express your feelings about it (e.g. your anger, resentment, anxiety, etc.)

3. Logically figure out your options for acting, listing all the likely solutions.

4. Work out a step-by-step plan of action.

5. Take step one. Act RIGHT NOW! Then,

6. DROP IT. Put the problem out of your mind. Pat yourself on the back for what you've accomplished and refuse to worry further. Turn your attention to something pleasant—like having fun.

Another technique is REPLACE THE WORRY. When you find yourself stewing about something specific, consciously shift your attention to something pleasant—*in the same general area of your life.* For instance, if you're worried about one aspect of your job (e.g. a meeting or deadline) turn your attention to an aspect of your job that you like (camaraderie, pay, creativity, sense of accomplishment). It's easier to replace a bad feeling with a good one than it is to stop worrying cold turkey. You need a positive place for your attention to go.

Or shift to a pre-planned happy thought ... something you anticipate with relish (a coming holiday, hot date, weekend, party, sports event, movie, book, concert, etc.). Then, when

worry strikes, switch your attention to the waiting happy scene. The worry will disappear because you can't think of two things at once.

DETOXIFY WORRY. If you fear worry itself, or worry about fear, take the sting from the words by repeating them twenty times, or until they lose their meaning and become merely boring instead of threatening.

The best distraction is usually to *move!* Do something physical or go somewhere else—anything to shift your attention away from what's worrying you. Whatever you do, don't fret in bed. Lying in the dark, alone and inactive, greatly magnifies worry because it has your full attention. Turn on the light, read, watch cheerful TV, or go for a walk. Do *any*thing to avoid lying awake at night worrying.

MAKE YOURSELF TALK. The sound of your voice will overpower worries. When you can't seem to shake them, make yourself talk about them—out loud. Put your worries into words. Bring them out in the sunlight and air them out. It will force you to focus on your problems. Explaining them out loud makes you organize, which often leads to easy, unsuspected solutions. It also makes your worries look silly, timid, irrational, and impotent.

Worst Scenario

If you're still stopped by worry, ask yourself, "What's the worst thing that could happen to me?" Take a cold analytical look at the very worst fate that could befall you if you dropped your serious (defensive) way of looking at life and wholeheartedly gave fun a chance. When you've figured out the most dangerous consequences, then soberly weigh the benefits against the drawbacks. Is protecting yourself worth all this agonizing? The answer should be a resounding "NO!" So immediately stop worrying and go find yourself some fun.

Maybe your hesitation involves worrying about what other people think, or putting others ahead of yourself. It's time to get selfish if you want to grow and change. Putting others first is a way of hiding out. Don't let guilt, shame, and unworthiness hold you back. The only way you can really help others is by being a good example. You can't change other people, and no one else can change you. So, "Do unto yourself as you would have others do unto you!"

The biggest gun in my arsenal is LAUGH AT YOUR WORRIES. Laugh at yourself for worrying. Laughter can shrink worry to nothing. To pave the way for laughter, sneer at your worries. Scorn them, disdain them, refuse to indulge them. There's no technique like laughter for turning disaster into fun.

Fighting Your Fears

While worry is likely to be vague and amorphous, fear tends to be focused and specific. It's defined as "anticipated loss," something you expect you won't be able to handle. When you're feeling afraid, you're not confident about your ability to cope.

The antidote to fear is trusting yourself. You need to build the belief that you *can* handle whatever comes your way. Success comes from doing the things you fear. The prescription is summed up in the book title, *Feel the Fear and Do It Anyway*, by psychologist Susan Jeffers (Fawcett, 1987).

Fear, says Jeffers, is an inescapable fact of life, not a complex psychological problem. We all have fears, but happy, successful people act in spite of them. They see their fears diminish as confidence in their ability to overcome them grows. So, you don't need a shrink, you just need determination and a few sound techniques. You build confidence through a pattern of achievement. Fear declines as self-trust increases. You build trust by expanding your self-worth through success. The more you succeed, the more fun you'll have—as the fear melts away.

So resolve to take at least one small risk each day to build achievement and self-trust. (If you plan ahead you won't "forget," and you'll avoid a lot of needless worry!). For instance, call someone you're a little afraid of, make an offer that might be refused, speak up, confront, do something you've always wanted to do. But don't be a daredevil. Don't take physical chances or intrude on other people. Your "risk of the day" must expand your self-worth by making you feel good about what you've achieved.

Then back up your daily achievements with regular affirmations built around, "I can handle whatever comes." Your growing confidence will shrink your fears, widen your life, and open the door to unlimited fun.

So there you have it, an arsenal of weapons for attacking the various enemies of fun. Pick the strategies you need and give them a try. Be patient and give yourself credit, not blame. When you fail, forgive yourself and forget the failure. Pick yourself up—and try again. You'll find fun ready and waiting in the chapters that follow in dozens of proven amusing techniques.

6

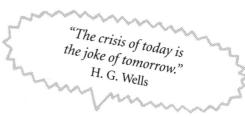

"The crisis of today is the joke of tomorrow."
H. G. Wells

Techniques for Generating Fun

Now for the many amusing techniques that will teach you to have fun whenever you want. Smiling and laughing, playing and joking, are delightful physical expressions of fun. By deliberately inducing them, you can change your mood and trigger the good feelings that turn you on to fun. So we begin with physical fun. Later, we'll work directly on the mind and emotions, returning to tools like "optimism" and "self-esteem."

We begin by dividing fun into common activities and locations, starting with the most private (home alone) and working toward the most public (your job) and the most intimate and vulnerable (sex).

Most techniques are simple and easy. Start with the most appealing ones; they'll probably be most effective. But don't duck the harder ones; you probably need them most. Begin with solitary fun, but go public—at least in a small way—as soon as you can. Let others see who you really are. Bring fun into your relationships—all of them. It quickly gets easier to have fun in public, because it's natural, vital, and appealing to others.

Fun at Home

The privacy of your home is the place to begin. Hopefully, there's nobody to watch or listen, so you can uninhibitedly experiment and make a little noise. When you're ready to bring your fun out of the closet, try what you've learned on family and friends—sympathetic people you can trust to laugh with you, not at you. Or just gradually slip fun into your life—without anyone noticing when the transformation started. People will find you're more fun to be around.

Fun in the Mirror

Start at a large, well-lighted mirror in your bathroom or bedroom. Get up close and study your face. You're going to teach it to smile and laugh. It's been conclusively shown (by researcher Paul Ekman, University of California, San Francisco) that our feelings are changed simply by mechanically changing our facial expressions. Smiling will actually lift our emotions. It doesn't matter if the smile is forced.

Happy mugging in the mirror—if you give it a chance—will raise your spirits and change your mood. You can induce fun simply by smiling, playing and laughing. So give yourself a big smile. Hold it for thirty seconds and examine it. Do you like it? If not, try changing it. Experiment with different styles. Copy somebody whose smile you like. Try more teeth. Lift those eyebrows. Open your mouth wider. If you're out of practice and your face feels stiff or you think your smile looks phony, some exercises are in order.

Open your eyes as wide as they'll go. Open your mouth till it won't go any wider, as though you were screaming. Feel the unaccustomed stretch in your lips. Practice winking and alternately raising your eyebrows. Stick out your tongue as far as it will go. Purse your lips and throw yourself a few kisses. You deserve them.

Society teaches us to be cautiously inexpressive, safely hiding behind a stony poker face or a glowering game face, keeping our feelings secret and hidden. But a defensive frozen face is the enemy of fun—and friendship. So loosen up. A mobile face is more youthful, appealing, healthier-looking and more fun to own. It takes forty-three muscles to frown and build wrinkles, but only fifteen to smile! Practice holding your best smile for sixty seconds.

By now, smiling should be easier. You should also notice that your mood has lifted and your feelings have changed. You've been oiling the hinges, chipping off the rust. You can probably feel the tingle and warmth of more blood in your lips. Now it's time to go further. Do some imitations of people who amuse you—friends, relatives, comedians, or celebrities. Include sound effects. Use your voice, hands, shoulders, and body. Doing Al Jolson's hands and Groucho Marx's eyebrows may date me, but they always make me smile. Impersonations dependably generate fun.

So make weird faces, throw kisses, puff out your lips to make them full, voluptuous, sensual and expressive. Mock your own seriousness. Poke fun, tease. Be coy, flirt. Mimic both men and women. Tease imaginary admirers, ape your friends and relations. Impersonate your favorite animals—puppies, cats, monkeys, koala bears, dolphins, bunnies, snakes—whatever appeals to you.

Pretend you're a comedian whose job is to make yourself laugh. Bark at yourself (that always cracks me up), hiss, growl, meow, woof, tweet, snarl—animating your face to match each sound. Concentrate on what you're doing, be passionate, wholehearted, and energetic. Push yourself. If you're starting to tire from the unaccustomed mirth, give it everything you've got for another sixty seconds, then quit. But by now it may be hard to stop smiling!

Laughter!

Now that you're having fun, and even if you aren't— "pleasure martyrs" may resist just to prove they can, clinging to defenses they're afraid to give up—it's time to step up to laughter. Your first laugh, like your first smile, may be phony and forced. Or all that smiling may have you chuckling already.

Laugh continuously for thirty seconds and notice how quickly it gets easier and better. That's because your body loves it; we love to laugh because laughing feels good, emotionally as well as physically. The only thing more infectious than enjoying yourself laughing is the sound and sight of other people laughing with you. That's why serious comedians get an assistant to 'warm up' the crowd before they start. They know that laughing is contagious.

So no matter how hard it seems at first, stick with it. If you force your laughter long enough it always becomes genuine. You never need a reason to laugh. Sixty seconds of hard laughter will usually prime the pump. When it starts to flow, it will lighten your mood and lift your feelings. That's the special wonder of laughter. It reproduces itself. So throw back your head and howl! Nothing will make you feel good so fast.

If you don't like the look or the sound of your laughter, do some experimenting. Change it. Laughter offers infinite opportunity for variety. Imitate laughs you admire. There are a million different laughs, but shy away from the polite titters, restrained chuckles and evil snickers. Studies show the most fun comes from laughs that can be described as "infectious, convulsive, booming, spontaneous, delicious, ecstatic, contagious, whole body, engulfing—real belly laughter."

We're talking about laughter that seizes you, takes your breath away, bends you double, chokes you, flushes and overpowers you, makes you gasp for breath, leaving you lost, red-faced, helpless, eyes watering, spent, while still giggling, cackling, or guffawing. That's what you're aiming for: the kind of laughter that gives you a whole body massage and leaves you gasping, happy as a child on Christmas morning.

So get serious about making yourself laugh! Make different kinds of faces, the more ridiculous the better. Talk babytalk, lisp, mince, get outrageous, make a happy fool of yourself. Wave your arms, mug at the mirror, move your body, jump up and down, yell, sing, tell jokes, scream if you want to, but *make yourself laugh.* You'll find the process as much fun as the result.

Try different styles of laughter. Imitate in turn the giggling girl, fiendish monster, country bumpkin, cool sophisticate, bubble-head, booming bear, lecher, cackling witch, and so on. Whenever you want to ditch the blues or find fun, go to the mirror to smile and laugh. It won't be long before all you have to do is remember your sessions at the mirror. The memories will make you laugh—or at least smile—if you let them.

Get Moving

Now that you know how to smile and laugh at will, it's time to get the rest of the body involved. Kids, you'll notice, don't restrict fun to their faces and vocal cords. Their whole bodies get involved. Now it's time to generate fun with motion and movement. Back away from the mirror, turn on a tape of stirring music, and march. You're on parade. You're the drum major of a marching band at halftime on big game day, so strut your stuff. John Phillip Souza march music is perfect, but anything with a strong beat will do.

Lift those knees high, lean back elegantly, chin in the air, swing those shoulders with the assurance of command. Keep time with your baton. Blow your whistle with authority as you make a snappy turn. Do an "eyes right" as you prance past the reviewing stand (your full-length mirror). Toss your baton high in the air, watching it spin lazily, catching it deftly an inch from the ground. Move to the insistent cadence of the music, proudly leading your band across the field in the wildly cheering stadium.

If you're female, you might prefer to be a cheerleader, keeping time to the music as you sway and prance and wave your pom-poms, cheering on the crowd, exhorting your team, feeling the engulfing emotion all around you. Jump and yell, dancing to the beat of the band, leaping for joy, going crazy when your team scores.

Now the music changes to a Latin beat, and you're leading a conga line of celebrants on New Year's Eve across a glittering ballroom. From marching we've turned to dancing, so feel the beat and move dreamily to the rhythm of the music, executing your favorite dance steps with flair, precision, and panache. Slink, strut, glide, spin, dip, pivot, bend, float, stretch, slide— "dance your ass off!"

Your only purpose is to release the pleasure of movement, the joy of rhythmic motion, to take advantage of music's genius for touching our feelings, opening up to fun. Studies show that nothing has the capacity to thrill us like music. Sex, by comparison, only rates sixth place!

These are just examples to get you started moving. Go with the images that stimulate you most, the people and roles that swing your mood toward fun. It's important as you experiment with smiling, laughing, impersonating, marching, and dancing to pay attention to what turns you on. You want to build an arsenal of images, movements, people, songs, animal acts, and rhythms that will dependably trigger a spurt of joy, a jolt of happy electricity, a sure-fire jump-start to fun.

Maybe it will help if you sing. I find singing love songs positively thrilling. Or dress up in fancy clothes or wild costumes—whatever it takes to generate fun. These sessions at the bathroom mirror, or marches and dances in a bigger arena, can be as simple or elaborate as you like. For some, they become a playful, intimate, personal, permanent, sustaining fantasy interlude—repeated daily or weekly or whenever they feel the need for fun. For others, they're merely a first physical step to opening the door to fun again.

Mental-Emotional Techniques

Sit down at your desk and put what you've learned so far on paper. The act of writing reinforces and highlights memory. In a large notebook write down the routines that brought you fun fastest: the specific faces at the mirror that made you smile and laugh, the imitations and movements that amused you most. This is precious information because just recalling it will bring back fun. It's insurance against gloom, protection from depression. No matter where you are, the memory will bring you a spurt of pleasure.

Using what you learned about what makes you laugh and smile, try to analyze your sense of humor. Search your memory to see what amuses you or makes you feel good. Make a list of what tickles you, e.g. a puppy chasing his tail, a favorite joke, a romantic interlude, or a dynamite vacation. If there are sure-fire scenes or situations that crack you up, catalog them to fall back on when times are tough. Keep them in mind to rescue your mood when adversity strikes.

Along with images and memories, collect funny photos, one-liners, slogans, punchlines, mottoes, (e.g. "You can't make ME mad!") cartoons, jokes, hilarious moments, and hysterical images. Conjure them when you're upset, knowing that if you can muster a weak smile and hang onto it, the mechanical act

(The Law of Smiles) will turn your feelings around. So stock-pile this gold for your lifeline to fun.

The ability to tell jokes is not essential to having fun, but it can help. I don't like telling jokes well enough to remember many, but I know people who tell them marvelously and I often enjoy listening. If you like jokes, they can be a great aid to having fun and making friends. A small stable of inoffensive jokes, written down, memorized and rehearsed, can be a valuable asset.

Even if you're not a joke-teller, you may want to experiment with less structured humor. Exaggeration is the basis of most humor, so it's the royal gateway to fun. If you want to be amusing and amused, learn to wildly exaggerate whatever's being discussed. Exaggeration is also a great technique for deflating your problems by highlighting their absurdity. Exaggerate enough and *anything* can be made to look ridiculous.

When the absurdity clicks into focus and you see the comic aspect of your problem, you can laugh—and feel the anger, pain, and sadness drain away. The more crushing the irony, the greater the hilarity. Exaggeration is what enables you to see the absurdity of your problem. So, look for opportunities to exaggerate, and practice. Wild exaggeration leads directly to fun.

Affirmations

Strong affirmations remind you of your goals. You need to believe you can change and have fun. Napoleon Hill wrote, "Whatever the mind of man can conceive and believe, he can achieve." But before conception comes desire. So first decide what you want, then conceive it through your collection of pictures, drawings, and photos. Commit yourself to believing what they tell you by composing and writing down strong affirmations.

Try: "I won't tolerate negativity." "My life is headed upward."

"I'll make fascinating friends." "I'm an incurable optimist." Create your own, plugging in your secret hopes and dreams, and try to phrase them as though they had already happened.

Belief is best generated through visualization, so try to imagine what you want. See it in your mind. Sometimes it's easier to construct a static scene, a fixed tableau, than it is to imagine an ongoing event. For some of us, visualization is easy, vivid, and natural. For others, it seems impossible, but it's not. If you have difficulty, try a private place secure from interruption, and close your eyes. Practice in bed after turning out the light. It's a wonderful time to imagine future fun. Plug into your daydreams. Embroider and savor them. They'll lift you and relax you and help foster pleasant dreams.

One way to keep your mind on fun is to put up signs. Get a packet of 3x5 cards and write yourself reminders, affirmations, and slogans. Tape them to the dashboard of the car, every mirror, the refrigerator, closet door, shower curtains, clocks, and windows; slip them into pockets, purses and wallets. For starters, try: "Think fun," "Why so serious?" "SMILE," "Too busy for fun?" "Be playful," and "How long since your last laugh?"

Or make yourself reminders of strategies that work for you, punchlines and one-liners that make you laugh, coming delights, etc. Keep yourself reminded that fun is waiting everywhere— if you're looking for it.

To keep your mind on fun, before you go to bed list twenty-five instances of fun you enjoyed that day. Then put down all the things you could do tomorrow that would be fun, and don't forget to include helping others.

Daydream. Look farther ahead to all the good times coming. Construct happy pictures of the future. Take your time and embroider them with coming delightful detail. Savor the anticipation. You're building a bulwark against the days when life looks bleak, a storehouse of pictures you can invoke as insurance against depression, armor against disappointment, escape from gloom. Collect them in your notebook for quick reference when they're needed.

At difficult times in my life, daydreams have kept me going. As a young man, I used to plan elaborate summer backpacking trips into the Sierra high country I love, seeing myself among the peaks, sitting by a campfire, catching trout from mountain lakes. I worked out itineraries on maps, planned menus, read books, and studied pictures of past trips. Looking ahead to those delightful summer trips, fastening on preconstructed images, brought me spurts of pleasure that got me through some difficult times. It let me enjoy the fun many times before it happened.

With an arsenal of daydreams you're ready for adversity. When things go wrong, if life seems hard or the weather stays stormy, just climb into a daydream and shut out the world. Put on rose-colored glasses and drift into the rosy future, dreaming of the wonders that lie just ahead.

Successful salesmen have a very effective formula for achieving any goal. It's called "Be/Do/Have." Here's how it works. BE what you want to happen (e.g. be happy). DO what you want to happen (do what's fun). HAVING fun then follows automatically, as a result of the Being and Doing.

Take Your Fun on the Road

Armed with an arsenal of techniques, a new attitude and determination to have more fun, it's time to try fun in public. When I go walking or shopping I take advantage of every shop window, mirror, or other reflective surface to play games with my reflection. I make faces, wave my arms, do brief imitations. The risk of getting caught just adds spice. They can't put you in jail for that kind of mugging. The funny looks I get crack me up. Recalling some of them now makes me laugh.

Make a commitment to yourself to find five occasions to smile in the next hour, and on two of those occasions resolve to laugh. It will lighten your day. Work your way toward extending your resolution to smile and laugh during *every* waking hour. It's easier than you imagine. When you discover that it's fun and that people like you better, it takes less and less effort to build the fun habit.

As I walk, I look for ways to play. I swing my arms, hum tunes, smile at passersby, and seize opportunities to speak cheerfully to others—for me, not for them. If I pass a children's park, I stop to swing on the swings, talk to kids (and their mothers if they need reassuring), bounce on the teeter-totters, slide down the slide, play on the bars and rings. Little kids watch me open-mouthed. I love to watch the natural way they move. They find ingenious, imaginative ways to have fun. I never pass up a chance to talk to unspoiled kids.

If you want to learn about fun from an expert, spend time with a child who hasn't lost the knack. Offer to watch your nephew some Saturday, accept a picnic invitation that includes kids, babysit, go to the zoo, or spend a few hours in a children's park. Playschools and preschools are perfect. Fingerpaint, mold Play-Doh, run through the sprinkler, build castles in the sand, draw pictures, play with shadows, mimic animals, make puppets. If you're rusty, the kids will eagerly show you how. If your mind is open and you forget your dignity, you're sure to have fun—and maybe learn to be silly and playful again.

Kids know it's natural and feels good to touch. See how unselfconsciously they hold hands, wrestle, lean and rub against each other, playfully push, grab, and shove. They're not afraid of closeness and contact, and they show their affection physically. Adult touching can be just as natural and rewarding, because it's fun and appropriately expresses affection. Try it.

Start with loved ones and children to build experience and confidence, then work your way toward friends, distant relatives, even strangers. Be sensitive to the responses you get. They're a dependable guide.

If your touch springs from genuine feeling—and isn't forced or sexual—it will be received with gratitude as a sign of affection. Master the gentle hug, the playful shove, the firm arm or shoulder squeeze, pat on the hip, slap on the back, quick rub, hand squeeze, chuck under the chin, brush of cheek, bear hug, arm around the shoulders, pristine kiss, friendly lean, casual stroke or massage. Spouses, kids, and lovers can be more openly affectionate, sitting on knees or laps, holding, stroking, kissing, caressing.

Don't be afraid to make your touch firm, or to touch members of your own sex. If you're out of practice, contact may seem awkward at first. You may feel vulnerable because you're offering intimacy. Experiment on where, when, and how to touch. Be genuine, follow your heart and trust your instinct and you won't go wrong because we all need and like innocent affectionate touching. If you're phony or overdo it or get sexual— you'll know by the reaction you get.

Affectionate contact brings both parties pleasure. To touch someone is to intimately offer evidence of your affection. Touching has been shown to stimulate health. Infants and children need it desperately in order to thrive. Every conceivable health benefit (slower heart, better skin tone, lower blood pressure, reduced muscle tension) has been attributed to frequent physical touching. We all need it—more than most of us know!

I never pass within arm's reach of my wife or daughter without reaching out to touch them. And I touch most of my friends, and strangers I like. It's fun and it expresses and reinforces the affection I feel. If you don't like to touch or be touched, recognize that you have a problem—and that you're missing out on one of life's pleasures. Make up your mind to overcome your inhibition by experimental touching. That's all it takes to learn the fun of contact.

More Physical Fun

Running, jumping, and skipping offer other physical ways to generate fun. In the country or wilds, alone or with my wife, I'll lie in the grass, feel the outdoor textures, hug trees, climb rocks, swing from limbs, exploring like a child, enjoying the natural world. Because it's fun. If I have to wait in line I make up stories about my companions, flirt with babies and young children, or daydream about the future.

Exercise that's playful converts physical motion into fun. Vigorous movement that drives and tests the body provides sensual stimulation that yields a feeling of well- being. You don't need the competition of organized games. If you're a sedentary type, you're missing out on fun—*and* good health. Just fifteen minutes of exercise a day will make you twenty percent less vulnerable to heart attacks, and forty minutes a day raises that to 40 percent.

Walking a mile or two will markedly reduce your anxiety level, boost energy and optimism, and cut anger, depression, tension and hostility. By distracting and refreshing you, exercise can pave the way for fun. (See my Ten Speed Press book *Dayhiker* for details.) You can also joyfully dance, skate, swim, play frisbee, or romp with your kids without the curse of competition. I often take a break from the word processor to wrestle or chase my daughter when she sneaks up behind me to tickle me or cover my eyes.

Attitude is Everything

A happy mental set is the key to letting go and having fun. There are a variety of ways to mentally break down the barriers and tease yourself into opening up. No technique is so powerful as learning to see the humor in your troubles, the mirth potential in misery, because it turns your worst moments into some of your best. Laughter dependably reduces disaster. As Bill Cosby put it, "If you can find the humor, you can survive anything."

People who laugh at their setbacks no longer feel sorry for themselves. It's a matter of fighting fear by finding fun. Humor is a powerful coping mechanism. A largely unknown tool, it lies dormant and neglected within each of us. If you prefer pleasure to pain, decide to change your attitude. As the Johnny Mercer song of the 1940s insists, "You've got to ac-cen-tuate the positive, e-lim-inate the negative, latch on to the affirmative. Don't mess with Mister In Between!"

Unfortunately, negativity dominates our society. Happy endings are frowned on. The media is full of misery. Our culture has a monster attitude problem. Fortunately, you don't have to buy in. Simply turn your back on the media, especially the violence and disaster of TV and the press. You don't need bad news, but that's mostly what you get. When you find yourself criticizing someone, make yourself find two admirable qualities you can praise. See the object of your scorn in a golden spotlight that brings out the best in them. Looking on the bright side opens the door to let fun in.

Collect happy pictures that depict your idea of fun, and fill a bulletin board. Your travel agent has lots of alluring free brochures. When you need cheering up, go gaze at your Fun Board, getting lost in the delightful detail. It will bring back the dream and remind you to anticipate your rosy future. You can create more personal pictures by dressing up and taking photos of yourself making silly faces, spouting nonsense, being foolish—having fun. Let the pictures show how you want to be—happy, carefree, laughing and relaxed.

Meditating on the fun you want can also bring it closer. Find a quiet, dark safe place (like your bedroom) where you feel secure. Close your eyes, take half a dozen deep slow breaths and tell yourself to "relax, unwind, slow down, let go." Repeat this litany until you feel yourself relax, become still, and open up. Listen to your breathing, feel your body loosening. When you've let the world go, start conjuring images of yourself having fun. Imagine and anticipate in slow delicious detail. It's almost more fun than the real thing!

Do you embarrass easily? Escape the chagrin by training yourself to laugh. It's the ultimate defense in embarrassing situations, and it converts a painful situation into fun. You simply resolve to immediately laugh loudly whenever you foul up, fall down, fail, or feel foolish. Follow up the laughter by joking about your goof, but be careful not to put yourself down. Be humorous and gentle, human and imperfect, instead of serious, embarrassed, and defensive. "If you can laugh at yourself first," says an old Jewish axiom, "others are more likely to laugh *with* you than *at* you."

So when disaster strikes and you're tongue-tied with embarrassment, buy time with a big laugh, even if it's fake. Before you're through it will be real. But it has to be big and it has to be immediate. Weak or hesitant laughter betrays your embarrassment. Program yourself to react to disaster with a booming laugh, no matter how stupid, stung or helpless you feel. You'll cheer up twice as fast ... and get back to having fun.

Truly, every cloud has a silver lining. Every loss leaves a void that's a golden opportunity. That's just basic optimism. There's no greater asset for the fun-seeker than optimism, no bigger impediment than pessimism. So let's review the difference. The pessimist views trouble as permanent, hopeless, and inescapable. The optimist see it as merely temporary, limited, external, and not his fault. To rate your optimism level, ask, "How do I feel, think, and act when I fail?" If you're hopeful you're optimistic. To feel helpless is pessimistic.

To build optimism, make use of these four sure-fire techniques.

1. Listen to your inner dialogue. Unearth the pessimistic thoughts that produce the bad feelings that lead to your negative beliefs.

2. When you can isolate your negative beliefs, you can begin to change them by vigorously arguing against them. Vehemently deny, dispute, dismiss, let go, protest, and reject them.

3. Demand evidence of their accuracy, look for alternatives, check the odds, and question the value of your pessimistic beliefs. Then change your response to one of positive optimism.

4. When you isolate situations that threaten you, write them down, along with your new optimistic beliefs about them. Carry notes in your pocket for quick reference, or wear a string or rubber band around your finger or wrist to remind you. They'll help you remember the new way you want to react—optimistically.

Laugh at Yourself

Wise men know how to laugh at themselves. There's no talent more valuable. Nothing cuts the tension, stress and pain like laughing at your own misery. This morning, playing mixed doubles on the tennis court, everything was going wrong. My partner and I maddeningly lost point after point. "There's nothing left to do but laugh," I told my partner. She laughed so hard it made the rest of us laugh, and the tension was broken. After that, we played better—and had a lot more fun.

Nothing brings swifter, sweeter relief than the ability to turn pain into laughter. All it takes is the decision to laugh. The next time frustration strikes, instead of seething or screaming, try laughing at yourself. You'll be surprised by the delightful results.

Another way to find fun is to pretend it's your job to find the humor in every situation. Pretend you get paid for finding fun. And your pay is doubled when you find it in your own misery, absurdity, failure, or disaster. Anything that goes wrong is raw material, so you won't have long to wait. Use all the tricks you've learned so far to remind you of your quest.

You're going to discover what pessimists have never known —that fun is waiting everywhere. To keep you in the mood, it may help to read humorous books, listen to tapes, watch funny movies or even comedians. Practice taking ordinary situations and seeing how quickly you can find the humor—it's always there. Or use exaggeration to inject humor into the ordinary humdrum and routine.

Let Music Bring Fun

Since music is the number-one stimulant of feelings, it offers easy access to fun. It can make you sing, dance, tap your feet, nod in rhythm, conduct the band, keep time with your body, and march. Music lifts us when we're down, soothes us when we're upset, moves us to tears and laughter. The key is concentration. To generate feeling, you have to really listen. Background music doesn't do it. Studies show that passionate, classical music of the romantic period works best. Brahms is my favorite. Be sensitive and open to the stimulating effects of sound. They can generate fun.

Actively making music is more effective than passive listening. Playing an instrument is the very essence of fun. With my background as a singer, I like to break into song, hum, whistle, dance, or just move to the music I hear or sing in my head.

Try silently singing or listening to your favorite tunes the moment you awaken, just before you go to sleep, and anytime when you need a lift.

It always lifts my mood to jump into, "It's gonna be a great day," "Oh, what a beautiful morning," "It's a lovely day today," "Dream," "Happy days are here again," "Let's build a stairway to paradise," "Good day, sunshine," and various love songs. There are dozens, maybe hundreds, of others as good or better, because the only thing that counts is how a song makes *you* feel.

Our daughter keeps herself happy all year long by singing Christmas carols. She sees nothing wrong with singing Jingle Bells in July, so why should we? Songs you love can become great and dependable friends, ready at a moment's notice to lift your spirits, restore your mood, and generate fun, so collect and enjoy them. I have a small arsenal of-pick-me-up songs, melodies and snatches of music for different occasions.

Another source of fun that's surprisingly satisfying is helping others, especially as part of a group. Giving to others and the accompanying companionship make a wonderfully rich combination. They bring us the feeling of loving that we seek above all else. Generosity and kindness feel good. So do yourself a favor and help others. You'll find it one of life's sharpest, quickest, deepest sweetest pleasures.

Gratitude is the gateway to appreciation, our best definition of love. Kindness and generosity turn out to be our best expressions of gratitude. You'll find that they encourage the consideration you desire, banish negativity and make you feel good. Gratitude builds happiness—and vice versa. Gratitude is a feeling and must therefore be genuine, not forced or insincere. Generosity and kindness are acts. You don't have to care in order to be generous and kind.

Be generous, kind and grateful for the benefit they bring you, not to serve others. You'll find it's fun to find attributes to admire and appreciate in every person and event you encounter. Be accepting, allowing and approving because it feels good. Look for pleasure and beauty in all that surrounds you—in people, architecture, nature, music, drama and art—because it's fun.

A Better Sleeping Pill

Since fun is the key to relaxation, it can help you go to sleep. The secret is going to bed happy. Mug in the mirror while you're brushing your teeth. Park the day's cares and make yourself laugh to banish the enemies of sleep. It will lift your mood and let you truly relax. You can't buy a better sleeping pill than fun before bed. Once you snuggle beneath the sheets, envision a safe place you love and see yourself sinking into deep, restful sleep.

A two-word summary of this chapter is SEEK FUN. It's really all you have to remember. Look for fun in everything you do and happiness, success, and goodwill will follow. The best way to summon good feelings is to feel appreciation for everything and everyone around you. Gratitude, like generosity, feels good.

So there you have it ... a lifetime supply of strategies and techniques for generating a lifetime of fun. All you have to do is decide to HAVE MORE FUN! At first it may take some effort, but you can do it, and it's worth it. So pick the most appealing techniques and try them out—today. Don't postpone fun. Tomorrow may be too late!

I could give you a Daily Routine for finding fun, or a six or fourteen-day program, but it probably wouldn't fit your particular needs. People vary too much. Fun—and the hangups that block it—are highly personal and individual. Take a look at your strengths and weaknesses, then build your own routines from the techniques you need, making them as structured or as free as you like.

Nearly everyone benefits from mirror work, music, and a system of affirmations and reminders—especially if you're workaholic, fun-denying, angry, rigid, humorless, or overly serious. Developing self-esteem will be essential for the timid, fearful, humble, and undeserving. And pessimists, of course, need optimism—badly. The techniques you shy away from may be the very ones you need! But don't turn play into work. You're out to have fun, so don't forget to laugh at yourself. Laugh at your seriousness. Laugh your silly little troubles away.

With that advice, you're on your own. But whatever you do, stop often each day for just a few seconds to give yourself a quick shot of fun. You deserve it!

7

Fun on the Job

Turning work into play will put to the test what you've learned so far. Our attitude toward work is neatly summed up in the phrase "It's not *supposed* to be fun. That's why they call it work!" The principal obstacles to fun on the job are: lack of time, space, privacy, and control, not to mention the potential disapproval of competitive coworkers and superiors obsessed with production. You'll need most of the basic skills presented in Chapters Five and Six.

Specifically, you'll need optimism, self-esteem, and the ability to generate a fun-seeking attitude. And you'll have to be inventive, maybe even a little aggressive. Fun won't fall into your lap. You'll have to go after it. It will take determination, especially if you're shy, introverted, or easily embarrassed—and that includes most of us.

But it's worth the effort. "All work and no play makes Jack a dull boy." Finding fun on the job may be crucial to your health and happiness—maybe even to your life! Nowhere is fun more desperately needed, or in such short supply, because the time you spend working and commuting back and forth accounts for the major portion of your life.

So don't be one of those sad people whose real life begins when the sun goes down—people who do their living on weekends and vacations. It doesn't have to be that way. Your years at work can be endless hateful drudgery—or deeply satisfying and enriching. It's up to you.

The nature of your job doesn't matter in the least. Neither does your boss's personality. The only things that count are your attitude and firm intent.

At first glance, work and fun seem incompatible, if not mutually antagonistic. Traditionally, the workplace has been sadly serious, with no room for frivolity. Bosses and coworkers aren't known for their merriment. Too much fun on the job could be dangerous to your career. A pessimist would conclude that combining fun and work was patently impossible. Not so.

Our kind of fun is easy at work, because it's invisible. It lives in your head, well-concealed from public view. You can enjoy it in a crowd without offending or disturbing anyone. In fact, no one else need know it exists. Invisible fun is literally a life-saver, and it's just as valuable in any kind of relationship or interaction with strangers. But out-front fun is important, too. It wouldn't be healthy to suppress all expression of pleasure. Sometimes you need to laugh out loud and have fun in public.

So full-dimensional, deeply satisfying fun on the job means securing the cooperation of your superiors and fellow workers. But you can do it. Millions have. With patience, persistence, compelling evidence and help, you can sell all but the worst Scrooge on the newly-discovered virtues of fun in the workplace. We'll provide you with ammunition. It's well worth the effort to promote fun at work because it's far too important to do without all day.

Fun Pays!

Your chances today are better than ever of finding a sympathetic ear in management. Enlightened business managers everywhere are turning to fun and play, laughter and humor, in order to relieve boredom, increase productivity and build employee morale and loyalty. Because it pays. Besides designing their own programs, savvy managers are turning to a growing band of humor consultants. Their clients include Honeywell, IBM, AT&T, and other corporate giants. The dollar value of fun on the job has been discovered.

All work and no play makes for poor production. Companies with the most competitive (or repetitive or pressure-filled) jobs are increasingly turning to management- controlled, constructive fun to relieve tension and lighten the demands of the job. For instance, a maker of heart monitors, suffering serious production problems, offered fresh incentive to its employees. Every time a goal was met, a siren went off to stop work and a clown on a tricycle led the workers on a five to ten-minute plant-wide parade to celebrate. Thanks to these fun breaks, production rose to record levels.

The idea is to intrigue and amuse workers in order to reduce job anxiety and restore employee enthusiasm, creating a higher quality of life on the job. More fun raises worker performance and morale, reducing turnover and absenteeism. Other successful strategies include fitness centers, theme dress days, joke contests, ice cream socials, Halloween and Christmas parties, athletic teams, picnics, dances, and employee redecoration of their works areas—anything halfway reasonable that makes employees feel good about themselves and their jobs.

Sociologists in a 1985 study found that naturally occurring forms of spontaneous play at work actually helped get the job done faster and better, especially when the play took place at the beginning or end of periods when the work was slow or monotonous. Anything that produced fun and made workers feel like family stimulated production. Making work into fun is good business. No longer must work be destitute of pleasure, exclusively ruled by economic competition. As one researcher put it, "Pleasure perfects work."

One such purveyor of industrial fun is Matt Weinstein, Ph.D., president of Playfair, Inc., Management Consultants in Berkeley, CA. After watching his hour-long seminar for top executives on PBS-TV, I called Matt.

"Laughter is good medicine," he told me. "That's been known a thousand years. Nowadays everybody in business knows that shared laughter is the quickest way to relieve the tension caused by rapid organizational change. Constant change is frightening for most employees. They need help coping. Fun provides that help. Shared laughter leads to the shared values so essential to building a strong, fast-moving, flexible operating team."

Laughter, play, and fun are kinesthetic forms of communication (i.e. conveyed through emotional and physical sensation), Matt explained. They release valuable right-brain creativity, which is entirely different from the familiar left-brain talking and listening that make up 80 percent of business communication.

The old twentieth century model of business management based on Command and Control just doesn't work anymore. Rooted in overly rigid rules and roles, mindless repetition, and static relationships, it's hierarchical and slow-moving. And there's no place for fun, creativity, or play.

For twenty-first century business, Matt predicts, we're going to need the childlike kinesthetic virtues of spontaneity, optimism, creativity, and playfulness in order to survive in a workplace that grows more competitive each year. By the year 2000 there will be an acute shortage of qualified, skilled employees. To keep them content and attract the best replacements, managers need to start nurturing now by instituting fun and play on the job.

A study at the Long Beach School of Business found that people who saw their jobs as fun were more productive, creative, and closely bonded to coworkers than were employees who were satisfied with their jobs but admitted that they weren't really fun. Fun made the difference.

But the biggest reason for creating fun at work turns out to be the most human. "Look," says Matt, "over our work life we're going to spend more time with the people we work with than we do with our own flesh-and-blood families. If we can't create some kind of meaningful relationships on the job, we're wasting most of our lives.

"Fun is good business because people like to do business with people who *like* to do business—and with companies whose employees like to work there. It shows. Smart managers recognize and reward their people. Nobody gets enough positive feedback, so it's good business to take care of the people who work for you. If you do it with fun and play you get maximum impact. Rewards and fun build closeness, support, and teamwork. And the business of the future is all about teams. So putting fun to work is the best investment you can make. Fun is changing the face of American business."

And not a moment too soon. Corporate America is a highly stressful workplace. Fun and humor can reduce that stress, cutting down on illness and absenteeism, while increasing productivity. Consider a few recent examples.

Staid but embattled Bank of America conducted a joke and cartoon contest among its employees, widely distributing the winning entries on company bulletin boards. Another firm in difficulty produced a humorous music video to boost office morale. Eastman Kodak built a Humor Room at its Rochester, New York, headquarters so employees could unwind at work. Playfair issues its clients a Stress Support Kit, which includes a snap-on red clown nose, wind-up teeth that chatter and ball point pens shaped like carrots and dead chickens.

You get the idea. As you work and play your way through the rest of this chapter, consider what you and your fellow workers might appropriately propose to sympathetic managers where you work, to generate some institutional fun on the job. Company sponsored programs and encouragement can do a lot to lighten the atmosphere.

But you don't need permission to have fun at work. Don't wait for management to bring you fun on a platter. Having fun—wherever you are—is up to you. Many of the basic strategies in chapter six can be adapted to the workplace as well as to and from it. Nowadays the average employee spends several hours each day commuting to work by train, plane, bus, car, bicycle, or on foot. And a lot of that time is spent helplessly waiting, bored and ripe for worry and self-pity.

So the first step in bringing fun to work is (1) making commuting more fun. It will be followed by (2) strategies for use privately, (3) fun while actually working, and (4) fun in public.

Fun Commuting

If you're sitting on a train, bus or plane you can amuse yourself by examining your fellow passengers. Find the fun in their expressions and interactions. Imagine what they do. Make up stories about them. See them as animals or celebrities. Flirt with babies and young children. Personify objects and give them names and personalities. Recall jokes, amusing experiences (consulting your notebook or 3 x 5 cards).

Look out the window, intent on finding fun, intrigue, entertainment, or humor in the scenery rolling past. Be a humor scavenger. Be determined to find the fun in everything. See your route to work for the very first time through the eyes of a visitor from a foreign country—or from another planet—and mentally supply a travelogue.

Speak to strangers, look for ways to learn something new. Listen to favorite music or inspirational tapes on your tape player. Mentally sing and play, spouting nonsense, constructing puns. Read happy uplifting, humorous books. Write down ideas for future fun. Plan trips, dates, parties, and vacations. Kill time creatively. Close your eyes and daydream about specific delights to come in the future. Savor the delicious detail. Visualize and imagine as the miles roll by. Meditate on longer-range life goals.

If your commuting is less public (by car, walking, on a bicycle) you can be more expressive. There's nothing better than singing out loud to lift your spirits. Move to the music to express your happy feelings. Walking or bike riding lets you move with less restraint, using your arms and legs expressively. On a bike you can pretend to be a daredevil racer, bravely banking each dangerous turn.

If you're walking you can slip in a dance step, a skip or make an elegant turn as you hum. March to the stirring beat of Souza in your head. Smile or speak to passersby. Mentally assign them names. Personify objects. Greet dogs and cats. And don't forget to play games with your reflection in all the windows you pass, making yourself smile and laugh.

Smile at fellow motorists who look especially cheerful—or decidedly grumpy. Wave or nod when you catch someone's eye. Allen Klein in the *The Healing Power of Humor* tells of a very proper lady who amuses herself as she drives to work by throwing kisses and mouthing, "I love you" as she whizzes by startled drivers. Klein carries a jar of soap bubbles and blows bubbles out the window when he's stuck in traffic. He also dons a red plastic clown nose to startle and amuse fellow commuters. If you're gridlocked, borrow some of the stratagems of the plane/train/bus commuters.

Private Moments at Work

No matter how public the workplace, there are private opportunities for recharging your fun battery. When you're alone in the bathroom, never pass the mirror without a quick bout of mugging. Use your best routines to make yourself smile and laugh in a hurry. Move your arms and body. Imitate your coworkers. Impersonate the boss. Physically release pent up feelings and stress. Unload tension by expressing emotion. If it's hard to get the powder room mirror to yourself, go into a stall, close the door, sit down and use a hand mirror, or pretend to.

Empty corridors, stairwells, roofs, basements, closets, storerooms, elevators, darkrooms, empty coffee rooms, warehouses, parking lots, gardens, vacant offices, theatres, and other empty areas also offer privacy for quick, expressive bouts of fun to restore your good humor and release anger and frustration. When you're alone don't miss a chance to mug, march, skip, talk to yourself, prance, dance, hum, laugh, and play with every passing reflection.

If you're serving the public, you have an added opportunity to appropriately express your fun-loving, fun-seeking attitude. If you're selling, the opportunity is even greater. Customers respond to fun, often with their checkbooks. Never miss a chance to energize and restore yourself through fun. A quick fix in private can turn your mood around and rescue the rest of your day. If you let yourself go when you're safely alone, you can express a world of feeling in a matter of seconds. I've done it many times—with magical results.

Whistle While You Work

Jobs with privacy, freedom, and flexibility offer ample opportunities for fun, so we're more concerned here with worst-case scenarios. While you're actually working, it's often necessary to keep your fun and humor invisible. Although having fun is known to stimulate productivity, unenlightened superiors may tend to equate it with loafing on the job. So let's start with the inescapable: dealing with your superiors, keeping the boss off your back.

If the boss (or a customer) chews you out unfairly, don't steam and stew, do a Walter Mitty. Let your imagination turn the tables, deftly switching roles. See yourself as powerful and in charge. Play with the situation. Use your imagination to see the humor in the situation. Turn your tormentor into the appropriate animal (a shrew, pompous lion, harrumphing boar, prickly hedgehog, surly bear) or into an actor or comedian. Make him ridiculous, nonsensical. By turning things around, you lift your mood and keep his anger from reaching you.

If you're called on the carpet, hold tight to your sense of humor. Klein carries that red plastic nose in his pocket all the time. If he's being scolded he imagines what would happen if he casually pulled it out and put it on. Fingering a rubber proboscis in your pocket, it's not hard to visualize yourself casually picking your nose while the boss lectures you, or thumbing your nose at him, or sticking the plastic nose on him, then giving it a sharp tweak! Substitute, in your imagination, a fake mustache, lurid red lips, a toupee, glasses with bulging, bloodshot eyeballs—anything that amuses you.

Make a list of all the people who've irritated or angered you recently. Write their names on toilet paper, then take it to the john and use it, flushing your anger down the toilet.

Assign numbers to your favorite curses and four-letter words, then innocently speak (or shout) the number when you want to swear. ("Oh, FOUR!") It will off-load anger while it safely amuses you.

In the privacy of your home, catalog all the stressful, boring, unpleasant, monotonous aspects of your job in a highly exaggerated way. Parody them, reveal their ridiculous aspects, discover the absurdity. Then act them out in a wildly exaggerated manner.

Finally (still at home), protest your feelings in an old-fashioned temper tantrum. Stamp your feet, jump up and down, hurl pillows, slap the wall, scream and yell. Wave your arms. Blow off steam until you make yourself laugh. One of the few effective ways to deal with high job stress is to make fun of it.

If your work is more boring than stressful, experience it as a child might. Pretend you're doing your routine for the very first time. Explain it to a curious alien from another planet, taking pains to make it fresh and intriguing. Assign names to your tools, equipment, and surroundings. Give them histories and personalities. Personalize and personify. Carry on a dialogue with them. Create a private happy world inside your job. It can make your work an exciting adventure.

Or make your job into a game. Make up rules and scoring that provide suspense and excitement. Every kind of job can seem boring, even the most exciting, if you let it. But even the most repetitive can be made more exciting—if you make the commitment to transform it into fun. Make up songs, rhymes, and chants that fit the rhythms of your routine.

Use nonsense, slogans, mottoes and puns. Envelop your job in a secret fantasy kingdom of delight. Take a hard look at your routines, hunting for stimulation and ways to add variety. Question your habits and rigidity. Look for ways to inject fun. Switch hands, move furniture, decorate (or redecorate) your workplace. To lighten her afternoon chores our daughter Gellie sings

Christmas carols as she carries in firewood from the woodshed, marching to the music, playing a hopscotch-like game with her feet.

Does that give you ideas? Would balloons, streamers, or crepe paper help? What about wearing clown noses or funny hats? Or adding plants, fresh paint, happy art or cartoons? Management should be interested in relieving dangerous boredom and monotony, because it hurts productivity and employee morale. Ask for help—or at least support.

Do you wear the same boring clothes to work every day. Consider a change. Talk to fellow workers about holding a dress-up day, a costume contest. (At the party balloon wholesaler that sends out my faxes, the manager is always delightfully dressed for Halloween.

Give your fellow employees, customers, and superiors secret nicknames that amuse you (e.g. Fang, Cookie, Sour, Porky, Dogbreath, Teddy Bear, B.O., Grease). Put up signs, jokes, cartoons, and funny pictures in your office/workplace, bulletin boards, the coffee room, and cafeteria.

On Your Break

You spend a lot of time at work not actually working—at lunch, on coffee breaks, between meetings, running errands, etc. That's valuable time when you're free to have fun. Make the most of it. Never pass up a chance to get some exercise, especially if you're a desk worker. It can lift your mood to vigorously walk, play catch, toss a frisbee, even dance to Muzak.

When you talk to your coworkers, be cheerful, laugh, and smile a lot, keeping a twinkle in your eye. Keep an eye out for appropriate ways to have fun. Tease the gloom merchants, but don't get caught in their negativity. Be a bearer of good news, happy rumors, nonsense, and jokes. Be personal, vulnerable, give of yourself without putting yourself in jeopardy. Be spontaneous, optimistic, and caring. You'll make friends, win respect, and impress your superiors—maybe even win a promotion.

One of the biggest benefits of having fun at work is that it makes time fly. The hours race by when you're having fun—instead of dragging interminably. So when you've earned a break from work, make it work for you. Plan in advance for maximum fun. You'll cheer yourself up as well as your coworkers.

You'll find that fun also generates energy. Boredom, anger, self-pity and pessimism make time drag and steal energy. But fun energizes you—sometimes for hours. A booming belly laugh of less than thirty seconds can pep you up for the rest of the day.

So get up and tap dance on your break. Or tell jokes, do impressions, play the harmonica, draw portraits or cartoons, whistle or juggle. Use any skill or talent you possess to entertain. When coworkers applaud, ask for a standing ovation. You'll get it. If you haven't the skill or extroversion to entertain, do it in your mind, addressing an imaginary audience. See yourself on stage, the object of adoration. Let them hang on every word, hear them cheering everything you say. It will make you feel lovable and loved.

If you leave work on your lunch break, remember to treat every reflection as an invitation to mug and cavort. In a restaurant, joke with the waiter and your companions. Stop by a greeting card shop, or the rack at your newsstand, and read the humorous cards, looking for one-liners, punch lines, quips, jokes, rejoinders, hilarious exaggerations, and crazy art. Write down the best ones to share with coworkers, friends, and family.

Look for clever ways to work some of this new found humor into your work, to lighten memos, business letters, and communications of all kinds. Properly used humor is valuable, productive, and highly appropriate. It can make you vastly more effective. The busiest, most serious people can find time for a joke. One uptight office was lightened considerably by the presence one Monday morning of a smiling rubber goldfish in the water cooler.

One way to create humor is to pretend to take everything literally. Feign uncomprehending seriousness. Your deadpan response to cliches like "See ya around!" ("Around what?") will produce humor and fun, without offending anyone. Deliberate misinterpretation of platitudes and figures of speech is a form of exaggeration that reveals a sense of humor. It will generate fun and friendship—and make you feel good.

These are just a few of the strategies that have proven effective in generating fun on the job. Hopefully, they'll suggest a host of others appropriate to where you work. The intent is simply to demolish the many barriers to fun that haunt our workplaces. Clinical psychologist Jerry May of the University of Nevada's Reno School of Medicine conducted a study of fun's principal enemies. He found that the main causes of pleasure deprivation are low self-esteem, fatigue, stress, lack of time and money, too many responsibilities, and peer pressure.

I spent a pleasant afternoon talking fun with Jerry at his home in the mountains where we both live. Fortunately, all the enemies he unearthed can be successfully attacked by building optimism and self-esteem, by generating fun on the job, and by changing your attitudes and beliefs.

"Fun changes what we do, how we think and how we feel," Jerry told me. "It raises your energy and boosts your motivation to achieve. It calms you down, helps you forget your problems, and enhances creativity and learning ability. The most successful people tend to be those who have the most fun with their work."

All you have to do is start the ball rolling. The fun you generate will do the rest. Developing the ability to find fun on the job can turn your life around by transforming a sphere of your life that you hate into one that's richly rewarding. No investment is more important than discovering ways to find fun on the job for the rest of your work life. It can make the difference between success and failure, health and illness, wasted years and rich contentment.

Turning work into play is the highest form of fun.

8

> *"That's the most fun I've ever had without laughing."*
> Woody Allen (right after sex)
> in *Annie Hall*

Sex and Fun

Sex and fun have a lot in common (besides being three-letter words). Both are free-expression sources of pleasure and excitement. Both activities are intimate and vulnerable. Success in both depends on attitude and outlook. Both are victims of conflict between the strictures of society and our innate desires—producing anxiety and confusion. Both are punished by society by invoking shame and guilt. No wonder people are leery of sex and fun while secretly hungering for both!

Sex is *supposed* to be fun! If it wasn't, we wouldn't be here! The pleasure is built in to provide continuing incentive to procreate, thus insuring the survival of the species. Sex and fun should go together like moonlight and laughter. Sex can be a major source of fun, and adding fun to sex makes it infinitely better. If your sex life isn't fun, you're missing out on a lot.

But sex is usually anything but fun. Despite our brave, libidinous talk, sex tends to be deadly serious. Our puritanical society sees sex as bestial, clumsy, dirty, lustful, awkward, sinful, and downright ridiculous. Led by the church, our culture has stolen fun away from sex and replaced it with seriousness, shame and guilt. No wonder sex is fraught with tension and anxiety for most of us.

But there's no better antidote to tension and anxiety than fun. In fact, putting fun back in sex is the answer to sexual problems of every sort. Fun breaks tension and demolishes anxiety. It bridges the gap between intent and desire, generating genuine fulfillment. Adding fun to sex can rejuvenate, rekindle, renew, rebuild, resurrect, and revitalize any kind of sexual relationship. It can also enliven it, cure embarrassment, aid communication, dissolve stress, increase compatibility, dispel nervousness, promote relaxation—even restore orgasms, cure impotence, and aid reproduction.

The strictures and taboos of society try to make us forget that sex is perfectly healthy, normal, and necessary. We need to remember that our sex drive is strong to insure reproduction, even under desperate circumstances. It's normal to have a strong desire for sex, even though you're not procreating—even if you're not married! So don't cave in to society's disapproval. You deserve a satisfying, guilt-free sex life—even if it's only masturbation or fantasy. Whatever your sex urge, it's okay as long as it doesn't harm others. Add fun and you'll find it vastly more rewarding.

Bring Fun Back to Sex

Putting the play back in foreplay puts the fun back in sex by restoring balance and respectability to sexual desire. Sexual appetite is essential for needed closeness, touch, affection, contact, evidence of lovability, joy, physical warmth, play, procreation, and much more. But it's also fraught with peril. Never are we more vulnerable, intimate, naked, and revealed than during sex.

We engage in sex for a bewildering array of reasons, some of them neurotic (e.g. for status, conquest, power, and success). We invest sex with great symbolism, meaning, and importance, and we desperately pursue it for reasons we don't always understand. No wonder it's the repository of so much stress and strain. We joke casually about sex, but when it comes time for action, we're often deadly serious and tense. No wonder we frequently fail to find fulfillment.

Sexual fulfillment only comes from unabashedly claiming the satisfaction you personally desire—free from feelings of guilt and shame. You have to go for what you want, which means ignoring the powerful strictures of society. Fun can help supply fulfillment by liberating pleasure and releasing guilt and shame. So don't be ashamed of enjoying sex fully, and don't feel guilty about wanting it and needing it.

Don't Call it Love

In a desperate effort to make sex respectable, we frequently pretend it's an expression of love. But deep down we know that's often a lie—which drives the shame and guilt deeper. Be honest about your motives. Since a strong desire for sex is perfectly normal, you don't have to call it love when it's not. Don't compound your guilt by trying to deceive both yourself and your partner. Don't pretend it's love when it's good old-fashioned healthy desire.

Real love lives only in your mind and heart. Your sex drive comes from your body and emotions. Confusing the two can rob you of normal healthy fun. Turning sex into fun will wonderfully clarify your intentions. False protestations of love will only create more of the tension and guilt that you're trying to escape. (Note: I'm advocating shame-free honesty, not funless promiscuity.) Deceiving yourself or your partner will only dilute your pleasure. Honesty is essential for the self-esteem that allows real fulfillment. Without honesty, every kind of pleasure is denied. The more honest you can be, the more fun and fulfillment you'll enjoy.

Think of your sex partner as a friend with whom you have

fun in bed, a sexual playmate, a partner in search of healthy pleasure. Playfully approach sex as another form of fun and your chances of receiving (and providing) fulfillment will soar.

Fun Techniques

To begin—before sex—you need to get yourself in the mood for fun. Through deliberate decision you need to alter your attitude—typically tense and anxious—to enter into sex in a spirit of playful adventure. Putting to work the strategies you've learned in the preceding chapters will enable you to generate the fun-seeking mood that's essential. Basic techniques for optimism, self-esteem and changing feelings will get you ready for the bedroom strategies that follow.

From the start, keep it light and *talk*. Alleviate worry (i. e. anticipated anger) by talking to your sex partner about fun—beforehand if possible. Considerate talk is flattering. Try to communicate your fun-seeking attitude in advance, in order to obtain a reassuring response. Talk and playfulness are both turn-ons. So is considerate kindness.

Try to get your partner in a playful mood, ready to join in, by putting play into your foreplay and talking about your hopes and feelings. Aim to make the fun mutual. Candid conversation, reinforced by lighthearted, joyful, guilt-free touching and caressing will generate rapport. Try to avoid seriousness, urgency, tension, impatience, implied criticism, pressure, distraction, questioning, anxiety—any kind of stress or sign of hurry.

From the very start be playful, antic, funny, and amused. Let body language help communicate your mood. Wiggle, stretch, make faces, prance, nibble, nuzzle, strut, tease, and gently tickle (with your hair, clothing, nose, and toes, as well as your fingers and tongue). Sex therapists agree that there's nothing so sexy and effective for setting mood as a good strip tease—

but make sure it's pure fun by avoiding any hint of seriousness as you sensuously, slowly, tantalizingly, mysteriously take off your clothes.

Put on a floor show that will get your partner in the mood for fun as well as sex. Mug, dance, throw kisses, rub, stroke, and caress yourself, make rude and sexy noises, rock rhythmically (with or without music). Keep it sexy but light. Model funny hats, try on your partner's clothing, mock seriousness, sing, talk nonsense, mimic, purr, growl, joke, pun, hum. Make your tongue dance. Make fun of yourself (but never your partner), and never put yourself down. Lively upbeat music makes sensuous stripping more fun, and the soft light of candles keeps it sexy and mysterious.

After you're in contact—in bed or wherever—rub noses, tickle as you stroke and caress. Hum while kissing, licking, and sucking. Tickle with your nose, your hair, a feather, your toes, tongue, and breath as well as your finger tips. Gently pull hair, pinch, and bite. Continue to make faces, flirt, laugh, wiggle, and play with your partner. And above all talk. Maintaining communication is almost as important as staying playful. Sex quickly gets serious, urgent, and tense when it's deadly silent.

Make rhymes, use pet names, talk nonsense, be silly. But above all, communicate your feelings and desires. Sexual fulfillment comes from getting what you want, so don't be afraid to ask or gently assert yourself. Don't hide your desire behind modesty or false dignity—or some imagined duty to first satisfy your partner. Doing so only reveals your insecurity, shame and guilt. So gently, playfully, ask for what you want. Also ask what your partner likes, and offer to take turns and trade favors.

Tell your lover what to do to turn you on and make you laugh. Make a reciprocal agreement. Don't wonder or guess because you're too embarrassed to ask. Take the responsibility to communicate. Fun and candid conversation lead straight to sexual fulfillment ... and more fun. Playfulness and communication will multiply your passion and performance exponentially ... and convince your partner that play really does belong in foreplay.

Think of the strategies above as a pool of ideas to be skillfully drawn from—as appetizers, embellishments, spontaneous expressions, not separate scheduled events. Don't try to use them all at once.

Pick out a few that sound like fun and stand a good chance of amusing and stimulating your partner. Tune in to his or her mood. Use them naturally and spontaneously. Play around and experiment. Don't build a predictable routine. Variety is the spice of sex as well as life. And remember, the fun must be an honest expression of your feeling, not phony tricks whose purpose is merely to seduce.

The idea is to randomly, spontaneously scatter fun into every sexual encounter, using it like salt and pepper, according to your mood and that of your partner. Above all, keep sex natural and affectionate. Sex is such an intimate and vulnerable interaction that we're all highly sensitive and easily threatened. So start slowly, determined to be playful and convey a fun-loving attitude. Get in the mood, beforehand, then be yourself and trust your instincts. Self- trust, remember, is the antidote to fear.

When you treat your lover to a playful mood, you're giving something extra, a pleasant surprise, the intimate gift of yourself. Fun in sex isn't something you program, plan, or rehearse. Let the spirit of fun propel you. But be sure to plan your mood in advance. Deliberately summon a fun-seeking attitude and gently convey it to your lover, inviting his or her participation. Go easy at first, but try to tease your partner into joining in the fun.

It's not what you do, it's how you do it that counts. Success—for both of you—will depend on the attitude you create and project. So be clear about your intent, remembering that it's okay to have sex just for the fun of it. To maximize fun you need privacy, ample time, and freedom from pressure or distraction. Talk ahead of time about your desire to bring gentle, affectionate play into the bedroom—*before* blinding passion strikes. To avoid misunderstandings and possible hurt feelings, explain the difference between dull, serious routine sex and the affectionate seriousness you feel for your lover.

One of the biggest benefits of injecting fun into sex is the improved communication between partners on every level that results. Adding mutual fun and talk will rejuvenate sagging relationships. Frank talk promotes fun, and fun greatly aids communication. When you're having fun, it's easier to let your partner know your intimate feelings about what feels good (when and how), and what turns you on (and off).

So be sensitive and experiment, take a chance on being intimate and vulnerable. Be natural and trust yourself—and you'll find the great joy that fun can bring to sex, deepening your relationship and turning one more area of your life into fun.

9

> "Man is the only animal that laughs!"
> William A. Moody, MD

Advanced (Ph.D.) Fun!

Finally, I want to offer a dynamite advanced approach to fun and success. Open-minded fun-seekers will find it powerful and intriguing. If you want the very best—the most dependable source of fun—this chapter should excite you.

Until now, our pursuit of fun has been relatively conventional, using an eclectic collection of widely accepted strategies and techniques. Now it's time to step up to something less familiar but more potent, an approach that can double your fun. It has for me. Unlike many of our beliefs, it's practical, proven, and totally consistent. Tens of thousands of determined fun-seekers use it—because it works!

Modern science tells us we look at the world through a pin-hole, seeing only a tiny fragment of what we call reality. What we think of as evidence and fact is really just vague sensory perception. We make judgements from the highly limited perspective of our own narrow experience—then regard those judgements as gospel. Our traditional action-based belief system has more holes than swiss cheese. It's awash with inconsistencies which we vaguely shrug off as accident, chance, luck, and fate.

In stark contrast, the belief system that follows is concrete and comprehensive. And you needn't accept a word of it on faith. You can easily test it in privacy, at your leisure, without the slightest risk. It's based on the scientifically proven contention that each of us builds our lives, brick by brick, with our thoughts, not our actions. In other words, you are what you think, not what you do. Your thoughts, not your actions, determine the course of your life.

We all were brought up on the belief that "Actions speak louder than words." But modern science says it's the other way around. Words (and thoughts), it turns out, speak louder than actions! What you think and talk about most is what you get. We're all familiar with the phrase, "His worst fears were realized." Exactly! The balance of your attention—and intentions— direct the course of your life. No wonder our actions don't reliably produce the success that we seek!

The principal authority for this new belief is quantum physics, the foundation of modern science, which had its formal beginnings in the 1920s, building on the discoveries of Albert Einstein. Quantum physics explained the formerly inexplicable transformation of nonmatter into matter, time into space, and mass into energy. In the process it revealed that we humans have our origins in thought, not matter. Thought conceives both the body and mind. It's thought, not action, that drives human creation.

Human beings originate as a field of non material intelligence or inner awareness. It's this intelligence, propelled by thought, that produces what we know of as reality. The mind is now known to reside in every cell of our bodies, not just in our brains. Our cells all communicate with one another, thus creating the unfolding events of our lives. That's the scientific basis for creation through thought, not action. That's why our thoughts, not our actions, determine our reality.

The quantum view is easier to understand when you drop the distinction between body and mind and think of every cell as "bodymind." Bodymind permits the new world view that we create with our thoughts. We are thoughts that create bodies, not physical machines that have somehow learned how to think. Every thought you hold manifests in the physical body. The process doesn't take any effort. It's spontaneous. In fact, you can't stop it.

The balance of your attention determines what you get. Since thought alone creates, you alone are in control. That means you can be or do or have anything you want. Just understanding the process will get you started positively creating. To deliberately create, you only need to think about what you want. Persistent thought radically transforms the bodymind to bring you the fun and success you desire. Just put your attention on fun and feeling good—and you create it for yourself. It's that simple.

In recent decades, the findings of quantum physics have repeatedly been confirmed by independent discoveries of medical researchers and psychologists. And further corroboration comes from a wide spectrum of other sources—from ancient Indian philosophy to modern metaphysics. The result of this interlocking network of evidence is a new paradigm, a new view of the universe and the origins of man.

Deliberate Creation

Building more precisely on this new paradigm, it can be seen that deliberate creation of what's wanted will most dependably result from concentrated, passionate attention over time. Your life is a combination of what you most desire, expect, and believe. Thought acts like a magnet, continuously attracting what you focus your attention on, i.e. what you expect. Your expectations are based on your lifetime collection of beliefs. Those beliefs were formed by your interpretation of your lifetime of experience.

The process is continuous. You can't turn it off. You get what most occupies your thoughts. If you worry a lot, in time you'll create what you worry about! If your thoughts dwell on tragedy and disaster, failure and fear, you're in danger of attracting them! Garbage in means garbage out!

To deliberately create the life you want, it would seem that you need to monitor your thoughts. Since that's next to impossible, it's fortunate that there's a shortcut. Simply pay attention to your feelings. They're your dependable guide to the desirability of your immediate thoughts. Good feelings create success of every kind. Bad feelings lead to failure, illness, and despair.

Whenever you're having fun or feeling good, you're positively creating what you want. You not only achieve the bottom-line goal of feeling good and having fun, you're also generating every other kind of desired success. When you're feeling bad or giving attention to negativity, you not only don't feel good, you're attracting the opposite of what you want. That's why fun is so vitally important—as well as pleasant. It's both the means and the end. When you're having fun, you're also creating the success you desire! So you can't go wrong with fun! And when you have it, nothing else matters very much. You just want to keep on having fun.

Quantum physics has discovered that we don't really accomplish much through action, work, and struggle—unless our thoughts are in harmony with our goals—because it's thought that's doing the creating! Focused attention—repeated passionate desire and expectation—is what creates success or failure, not action, work and struggle.

Since we alone create our lives, we have to accept total responsibility for our actions. But by the same token, we're wonderfully free from the influence of others. No one else can affect our lives, unless we let them. Once we learn to protect ourselves with positive thoughts, we have nothing whatever to fear from others. We're safe! And since others are the sole creators of *their* own lives, we can't really help or hurt them—freeing us from the responsibility of looking after them.

So it isn't any sin to be selfish, as long as we aren't cruel or unkind. In fact, most of us desperately need to be more selfish, focusing our attention on our desires, well-being, pleasure and welfare. Don't worry about what other people think. You can never please everyone, and your failure will only make you feel bad. To find fun, you must learn to appreciate yourself, look within yourself, build self-esteem, and forgive and forget your failures. Live in the present, learn to laugh at yourself, take credit for your successes—and you'll be free for full-time fun.

Harnessing the Magic

Since you're totally free to be or do or have anything you want, doesn't it make sense to put the powerful attractive power of thought to work *for* you—instead of letting the sea of negativity that surrounds you work against you? Directing your attention to what you want, and avoiding attention to what you don't want: that's deliberate creation. And it's driven by fun. It not only creates the fun that you want, it can bring you all the other successes you desire—as well as good feeling! What could be better than that?

How do you use deliberate creation to generate big time Ph.D. fun?

1. Let this fresh evidence of fun's power help you break down the barriers that block your access to fun.

2. Give yourself permission to make the pursuit of fun high priority in your life.

3. Pay attention to your feelings, so you're aware of what you're attracting.

4. Think about fun—and everything else—in the most positive possible terms, and,

5. Let your positive thoughts act like a magnet to attract everything you want.

Passionately desire, intend and expect to have fun—and it will come. The more emotion you can muster, the quicker and stronger the results. That's the formula for deliberate creation according to quantum physics. Modern metaphysics (the systematic investigation of ultimate reality) holds the same basic view, but it goes one step further. It claims that each of us possesses within us a wonderfully wise inner self whose sole purpose is guiding us to happiness, growth, success, and well being.

Your Guidance System

The inner self guides us by pointing out the paths that will bring us the joy and success that we seek. It communicates with our consciousness through our feelings; its messages come coded in the form of emotion. At every crossroads, say metaphysicians, there are subtle guideposts pointing in the direction of joy and success. Reading the message is simple, but not always easy. When you feel really good, you're on the right path. Choices that don't feel good risk sickness, unhappiness, and failure.

To make your guidance system work, you just need to be aware of your bedrock feelings when you face a decision. The better you feel, the stronger and clearer the message from within. Belief in your guidance system will build trust in your ability to make the right decisions. Self-trust bolsters self-esteem, which in turn builds optimism, fights fear and your dependency on others, bringing confidence, comfort, freedom, and independence.

How do you build belief in your guidance system? You test

it. Forget about the unfamiliar source. See if the system works. When you're standing at the crossroads, considering a choice, pay attention to your feelings as you mull your options. Then see if the choice that made you feel good, deep down, leads you to success and continued good feeling. But don't expect booming messages or neon signs. And don't make it into work. Just relax, open up and go about your life, striving to feel good, thinking about the success you desire.

Instead of looking for magic messages, be alert for the warnings that bad feelings bring. Be suspicious of any course of action you need to rationalize or explain. Pay attention to warnings in the form of blockages, difficulty acting, and action based on "shoulds," blame, anger, worry, resentment, self-pity, "what-ifs"—or any other bad feeling. Negative feelings disconnect you from your inner self. When you're feeling bad you pull the plug on your guidance system. When you resume feeling good, you're connected again. If your system doesn't work, maybe it's because you're not plugged in to good feelings!

A personal guidance system is the perfect compliment to the new paradigm, because it builds comforting self-confidence in your ability to cope with whatever comes your way. How can you go wrong with a seer in your pocket?

The new paradigm may be difficult for many, since it's the opposite of the action-based beliefs we've known since birth. That's why I'm explaining it more fully in a sequel to this book that will show you ... *How To Have Everything You Want* ... *And Feel Good! (No kidding!)* [copyrighted title]. If you want to know more—right now—about harnessing thought for the deliberate creation of fun and success, just turn to Sources.

As you learn to use this potent Ph.D tool, the dark clouds of worry and negativity will lift to let the sunlight of fun and success shine through.

I wish you happiness and joy—and a life full of fun!

Fun in a Nutshell!

Decide there's going to be more fun in your life.

Know you can create it by changing your feelings.

Get serious about fun. Make it top priority.

Be an optimist. Expect the very best from every situation.

Learn how to be playful by watching unspoiled children.

Live wholly in the present. Forget past failures. Refuse to worry about the future. Focus on finding fun in every moment.

Seek freedom by being entirely yourself. Free yourself from what other people think. Rely on your wise inner self for strength and guidance.

Trust your judgement. Appreciate yourself. You can't love others, until you learn to love yourself.

Don't judge or fear others. They can't harm you unless you let them. Allow other people to be themselves. If you can't appreciate them, turn your attention elsewhere.

Be grateful, generous and kind—for yourself, not to serve others. Gratitude is the gateway to finding love. Kindness and generosity best express your gratitude.

When adversity strikes, forgive your failure and gently laugh at yourself. Forget disappointment and look anew for fun. You deserve it.

 HAVE MORE FUN!

Refuse to accept fun-killing blame, shame or guilt.

Know that fun is all around you, even in your darkest hour. If you're looking for it, you'll find it every time.

Understand that you need and deserve endless fun—as long as you're not deliberately harming others.

Fun is eagerly awaiting your choice.

All you have to do is lighten up and let it in.

Sources

In addition to the many sources briefly noted in the text, I want to recommend the following:

For greater understanding of the metaphysical beliefs set forth in Chapter Nine, along with dynamite advanced techniques for creating fun and success—including the concept of the wise Inner Self—I recommend two books: *A New Beginning I* and *A New Beginning II* ($9.95 each plus $3.15 S/H), available from Abraham Speaks, P.O. Box 690070, San Antonio, TX 78269. Phone: 210-755-2299. These books are clear and simple—but wise and profound—guides to a life full of fun and good feeling.

When ordering be sure to ask for the exciting free *Introductory Tape* ($2.75 S/H). *It could change your life.*

To learn more about quantum physics as the basis for healing and creation through thought (as opposed to action), read *Quantum Healing,* by Deepak Chopra, MD, an inspiring blend of neuroscience, Eastern and Western medicine, physics, and metaphysics (Bantam New Age Books).